Tuinkunst

2 · 1996

Edited by

 ERIK DE JONG

Assisted by

H.J. SCHEEPMAKER

Tuinkunst

Dutch Yearbook of the History of Garden and Landscape Architecture

ARCHITECTURA & NATURA

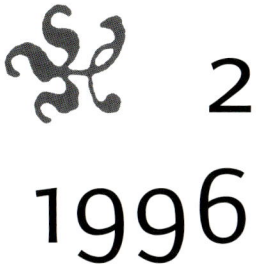 2
1996

Garden Art · Dutch Yearbook of the History of Garden and Landscape Architecture is published by Architectura & Natura International Booksellers, Amsterdam, to promote research into the history of garden and landscape architecture being conducted at the Free University Amsterdam, Wageningen Agricultural University, and elsewhere. Dr E.A. de Jong of the Free University has been appointed chief editor for the first four years.

Restoration of Baroque Gardens was financially made possible by the Netherlands National Commission for UNESCO, the Dutch Foundation of Architecture, Kragten Tuin- en Landschapsarchitectuur *Blaauboer Kragten Snelder*, Camille Oostwegel Château Neercanne, and the customers of Architectura & Natura International Booksellers.

Cover illustration   Isaac de Moucheron, The parterre in the garden at Castle Heemstede, with its triumphal arch and open-air orangery in the background, pen and watercolour 1700/1701 (Teylers Museum, Haarlem).

Copyright © 1997 Authors and Architectura & Natura.

Redactie Dr E.A. de Jong (Vrije Universiteit)
Tekstredactie H.J. Scheepmaker

Typografie Alje Olthof (†) voor de basis lay-out en Cédilles, Amsterdam

Produktie Offsetkopie, Hoofddorp & Waanders Drukkers, Zwolle

ISBN 90 71570 76 2
ISSN 1384-5721

Uitgave Architectura & Natura
Leliegracht 44
1015 DH Amsterdam
Distribution outside the Netherlands
IDEA Books,
Nieuwe Herengracht 11,
1011 RK Amsterdam

2
1996

Proceedings of the International Conference on
Neercanne and the restoration of Baroque gardens,
organized by UNESCO, 27-29 September 1995

7   ERIK DE JONG *Amsterdam, the Netherlands &*
    FRITS VAN VOORDEN *Delft, the Netherlands*
    A garden in a landscape.
    Aims and limitations of the Neercanne Conference

11 ADRIAAN VAN DER STAAY *Leiden, the Netherlands*
    The language of the garden

17 FRIDY DUTERLOO *London, Great Britain*
    Neercanne: A status quo of history, research and design

31 ERIK DE JONG *Amsterdam, the Netherlands*
    Neercanne Castle and the Dutch garden tradition

51 FRITS VAN VOORDEN *&*
    BASTIAAN KWAST *Delft, the Netherlands*
    Neercanne: Towards a definition of a dynamic composition
    and its characteristics

61 MARK LAIRD *Toronto, Canada*
    'Original fabric' or 'original design intent'?
    The unresolved dilemma in planting conservation

79 PIERRE-ANDRÉ LABLAUDE *Paris/Versailles, France*
    The Park of Versailles. Projects and achievements

95 JAN WOUDSTRA *Sheffield, Great Britain*
    The design of the Privy Garden at Hampton Court

121 GÉZA HAJÓS *Vienna, Austria*
Terraced gardens in Central Europe from the fifteenth
to the eighteenth century: Problems of conservation

135 KJELL LUNDQUIST *Alnarp, Sweden*
The restoration of seventeenth- and eighteenth-century gardens
and cultural landscapes in Sweden

145 NILAN COORAY *Colombo, Sri Lanka*
The restoration of the gardens of Sigiriya, Sri Lanka

161 FRIDY DUTERLOO, BADELOCH NOLDUS,
SJOERD SCHAPER, ANNEGIEN SCHRIER
& DAPHNE THISSEN
The seminar: A summary of workshops and discussions

173 Programme of the international conference and
lists of specialists attending the conference

A garden in a landscape.
Aims and limitations of the Neercanne Conference

ERIK DE JONG &

FRITS VAN VOORDEN

THIS SECOND *Dutch Yearbook of the History of Garden and Landscape Architecture* appears in the English language. While its topic is Dutch and regional – the terraced gardens at Neercanne Castle in the southern part of the Netherlands near the city of Maastricht – its scope is international.

It is a collection of the lectures given by experts from Canada, France, England, Austria, Sweden, the Netherlands and Sri Lanka during the three-day conference on the Baroque Gardens of Neercanne Castle, held in Maastricht on 27-29 September 1995. It also offers the reports of the discussions during the workshops.

The main theme of this conference was finding the answers to the questions raised by a possible restoration of the terraced gardens at Neercanne, which date from about 1700. This involved the evaluation of a wide range of problems, such as the relationship between the garden and the cultural landscape, the significance of garden archaeology, the roles of planting schemes and maintenance, the function of geometrical design and architecture in the landscape.

The Netherlands National Committee for UNESCO, which organized the event, seized the opportunity to present the challenge of Neercanne as a Dutch contribution to the larger UNESCO project 'Les Espaces du Baroque', which aims at stimulating international knowledge, expertise and exchange of information. At the same time, the seminar elaborated on the ideas and concepts brought forward during another meeting, the symposium on the Authentic Garden, held in Leiden in 1990 and organized by the Clusius Foundation and a section of the United Nations and UNESCO World Decade for Cultural Development.

Both in Leiden and in Maastricht, the discussions concentrated on the all too often unknown heritage of gardens. What are we to do with, and how are we to solve, the problems presented by this delicate heritage? How to benefit, in the case of Neercanne, from ideas and solutions already tried out elsewhere? And since UNESCO embraces global issues, it was decided also to consider the experiences with the preservation of gardens in another culture, Sri Lanka. The splendid example of the Sigiriya gardens incidentally extended garden history with about 1,500 years.

A main issue of the Neercanne case was that it offered a varied group of specialists – landscape architects, designers, geographers, art and cultural historians, botanists, horticulturists, private owners of famous gardens, monument preservationists and archaeologists – an unusual occasion for intellectual exercise, although right from the start it was understood that the seminar would have to result in workable suggestions for a restoration or reconstruction of the Neercanne gardens.

Yet the actual scope of all this is much wider. The conference served as a mediator in attacking the problems that have to do with the meaning and future of our cultural landscape. In a time and age when 'nature' has a distinct magic of its own, the existence of cultural elements in the landscape is threatened by ignorance and lack of insight. The Dutch 'Natuur Beleidsplan' of 1990, a report of the Government on the future of Dutch nature and landscape, already stated that we have gathered considerable botanical and ecological knowledge but that the cultural dimensions are still largely unknown. This refers to, for instance, the history of our myths and prejudices regarding nature, or the Dutch traditions in landscape planning, design and horticulture.

For a better understanding of the cultural values of gardens and landscapes, this *Yearbook* offers a variety of articles grouped around the case study of the Neercanne gardens. We hope that it will make people realize that similar problems occur in other places and in other landscapes. We also hope that it will arouse more interest in the intimate relationship between landscape, nature and architecture, rather than cultivate the traditional antagonisms between these essential values. We expect that cooperation will gain from the innovative character of the Neercanne seminar as it manifested itself in particular during the extensive discussions between representatives of disciplines normally not used to the exchange of ideas. Projects such as these are necessary to stimulate the reassessment of the larger issues – the revival, management and preservation of our valuable historic cultural landscapes. This applies especially to the Netherlands, where the cultural dimensions of the landscape are once more under discussion, with respect to the reorganization of rural areas for the purpose of urbanization, infrastructural expansion, nature development and recreation. The discussions about the conservation of the Beemster polder, the military defence lines and fortresses of the provinces of Holland and Utrecht, the Dutch country estate and the Wadden landscape are evidence of an important awareness.

The present collection of papers is preceded by a discourse on the 'Language of the Garden' by Adriaan van der Staay, Director of the Social and Cultural Planning Office. In its wide spectrum of ideas, it embroiders on the themes of the Authentic Garden symposium, which was organized by Dr. Leslie Tjon Sie Fat, to whose memory this text is dedicated. With him, we lost in September 1996 an inspired botanist and garden lover, who was always ready to share his erudition with colleagues and friends. Work will continue on the foundations he laid.

We wish to thank the following persons and institutions for their help in organizing and welcoming the seminar in Maastricht: the Province of Limburg, the Municipality of Maastricht, the Foundation Neercanne Castle Gardens, and Countess Michel d'Ursel at Hex Gardens. As to its scientific aspects, the event was prepared by the Faculty of Architecture, Technical University Delft, the Department for Architectural and Landscape and Garden History of the Free University of Amsterdam and the Sub-Committee for Culture of the National Committee for UNESCO in The Hague. We are particularly grateful to Deana Sy-A-Foek, Secretary to the Sub-Committee, without whose energy much of this would not have been possible. At Neercanne, Camille Oostwegel was the perfect host for the whole duration of the seminar, thus giving a new meaning to the traditional ties between hospitality and country life. Thanks to Guus Kemme of Architectura & Natura, the lectures delivered at the seminar are now published in this second *Yearbook*.

Financial support for the organization of the event and for this publication was given by the Participation Program 1994-95 of UNESCO, the Stimuleringsfonds voor de Architectuur, the Province of Limburg and the Municipality of Maastricht.

With great expectation we look forward to the implementation of the Conference's results and the concretisation of plans for the garden, for which designs will be drawn up by Wil Snelder, project-architect at the office of Blaauboer, Kragten and Snelder, landscape architects at Wageningen and Roermond.

A. van der Staay *The language of the garden*

The language of the garden

ADRIAAN VAN DER STAAY

In memory of Leslie Tjon Sie Fat

EXPERIENCE SHOWS THAT people learn languages best when they are young. We learn our mother tongue effortlessly in childhood, and if one or two other languages happen to be spoken around us, we may learn them too. Later in our youth, we learn languages at school, and especially while travelling, as we immerse ourselves in another idiom and let its subtleties come to life. During our youthful travels we also encounter gardens, and their language comes to life for us too. I will be using the 'language of the garden' as a metaphor in this essay, hoping in that way to steer clear of people who see the garden as a mere collection of plants or an artistic embellishment.

The language of the garden comes to life for us in our youth, when the incipient life of the child meets the life of the garden. The garden is not a dead object. In fact, it has a double life, because it is at once an artefact of our creative urge and imagination, and something that has been shaped from living matter. So the garden as artefact leads its own existence. It passes through youth and old age, bloom and decay, seasons, transitions from daylight to darkness and from rain to dry weather. The garden reacts. There are few creations of culture that mirror life as directly as this one, because the mirror also lives and dies.

There is indeed a period when we intuitively learn the language of gardens, during our first encounters with them. At first they are mere fragments without much coherence. An orchard that looks different from a forest. A garden wall built of loose stones with ferns growing from between them. A fishpond by a monastery, whose rigid outlines form a mirror to interrupt and frame the billowing clouds and the undulating movement of the hills. These are garden elements, but they are still just symbols and words without grammar or syntax.

And then, suddenly, the garden is there in its entirety, the garden that con-

Nicolaas Bidloo (1674/75-1735), View through a triumphal arch towards an imaginary garden, functioning as a frontispice to a series of drawings, illustrating the garden Bidloo laid out in the suburbs near Moscow, Russia. Drawing, pen in brown, c.1730. (Leyden, University Library)

veys its meaning to us like a completed sentence, an utterance in a language we understand.

I don't want to bore you with holiday slides from my memory, but one of them shows how we discover the identity of gardens. It was in England, not far from Cheam. I fled there daily from my holiday lodgings to read books I had purchased in London. Day after day I sat submerged in the language of Edmund Spenser and the sonnets of Shakespeare. I have never again read them as I did then. My haven of refuge was idyllic. Along the walls on three sides of a garden were old, overgrown arbours containing stone benches. There were sturdy paving stones at my feet, a small lawn in the middle, and a view of a house that once belonged to Henry VIII. This brought home to me what a garden could be, a humanistic garden, a garden for Erasmus or Thomas More – walled in, peaceful, tranquil, with nothing to disturb my listening. Listening to the great passion of Shakespeare and the whispered verses of Spenser: 'Sweete Themmes! runne softly, till I end my Song.' Eliot quotes this paradisaical phrase in *The Waste Land*. The pieces fell into place and became one garden, the garden of humanism.

Just one more slide from my memory, from around the same period, the 1950s. The French are decolonizing Morocco and have all but withdrawn from Marrakesh. The city's ruler, Al Glawi, is tottering and will soon bow to a more modern prince. But his sixty-piece private orchestra still plays age-old Andalusian music and I wander through the gardens of his palace, my head swimming. I have just fled here from the sun in search of shade. Water flows in tiny rivulets from tree to tree, forming puddles around them. The paths are raised above the garden floor, and I am walking through a sea of flowers no higher than the path. I have entered a world of water and shadowy colours, while the outside world is grey with sunlight, until night falls rapidly. We learn here that the garden speaks not just one language, but several. The Humanist garden of the English Renaissance is joined by the Andalusian heritage in the Moorish gardens of Morocco.

So we learn that the garden speaks several languages. Perhaps there are more garden languages than dialects. As the intuition of youth gives way to the analytic gaze of the adult, we realize that this profusion of garden dialects can be classified according to place and time.

As regards place, we learn that the driving force behind the linguistic differentiation of gardens is called their *genius loci*. The geographical diversity of gardens derives from the spirit of the places where they are situated, from their characteristic properties. It seems that only those gardens that are based on this *genius loci* speak a powerful, enduring, hence classical language – classical gardens fit their sites.

At least that was how the greatest garden architect of our century, Russell Page, perceived it. 'But first of all, I must absorb as best as I can all that I see, the sky and the skyline, the soil, the colour of the grass and the shape and the nature of the trees. Each halfmile of countryside has its own nature and every few yards is a reinterpretation. ... I cannot remember a completely characterless site,' Russell Page writes in his invaluable *The Education of a Gardener*.[1] The *genius loci*, an interest in the limitations and opportunities that the garden's natural location prescribes, also permeates the work of Roberto Burle Marx, a great Brazilian garden architect, and rescues it from modishness.

Despite the accomplishments of these two and a handful of other garden designers of stature, the artistic avant-garde of our century has given scant attention to the garden, as Erik de Jong has observed in his introduction to the book *Aardse Paradijzen*.[2] This can be traced in part to a lack of interest in the *genius loci*. The modernism that influenced Western culture between, say, 1920 and 1970 was neither humble nor earthly. It was utopian, and utopias by definition have no eye for the constraints of the lie of the land and its *genius*. Furthermore, modernism celebrated the omnipotence of the designer and it had a Platonic character. I have commented on this in my book *Van Parken en Tuinen*.[3] This is why the good gardens of this century have been largely the work of eccentrics.

The problem of the *genius loci* inescapably pervades the best gardens that we see portrayed in this exposition.* The idiom of the Dutch garden is governed by its native Dutch language of struggle against wind and water. The Dutch garden speaks naturally in this mother tongue, in canals and ditches, walls and wind-breaks. In fact, the Dutch garden has a double *genius loci*. There is the garden of the city and the garden of the country – which in Dutch is inevitably called the 'flatlands'. There is the *genius loci* of cities squeezed together on tiny parcels of land, and there is that of the expanses of reclaimed land outside the cities. The language of the Dutch garden alternates frequently between the spacious and the snug. Venetian gardens have only the latter quality, that of intimacy, situated as they are in the vastness of the sea.

So far about topographical diversity. When the garden speaks, it speaks not only the language of the *genius loci*. It also speaks the language of tradition. The diversity of tradition is of a different nature. The effect of the *genius loci* is centrifugal; that of tradition tends to be centripetal. Both are restrictive, since we can only speak words we have learned, but the language of tradition need not be meagre.

Let me now venture a sweeping conclusion. Actually, it is not just *my* conclusion; you can also find it in a book such as *The Poetics of Gardens*.[4] From a global perspective there are basically no more than two great gardening traditions on Earth: that of Persia and that of China. Both have proliferated in the course of history into a wide variety of forms.

The West has drawn on the Persian tradition, the East on the Chinese.

We can recognize the Persian tradition in my walled-in *parterre à la Erasme* as well as in the Moorish garden in Marrakesh, so different at first glance. Villiers-Stuart, in her authoritative work *Gardens of the Great Mughals*, identifies again and again the language of forms that these gardens share with the gardens of Europe.[5]

This is the garden tradition of the present exhibition. The Persian tradition speaks the language of control and seclusion, the struggle against nature. Paradise is the antithesis of savage nature. It was this Western garden language that the Mughal rulers used to impose order and paradisaical beauty on the disorderly India. The conqueror and garden-lover Babur wrote in his autobiography that India lacked both charm and regularity.[6] This is a Western verdict. It is this same paradisaical control and seclusion that structures the gardens of Jekyll and Lutyens on the Atlantic coast. In the light of this dichotomy we might call the Taj Mahal the most unearthly paradise garden in the Western tradition, and we could find the most earthly form of paradise at the Villa Lante or in Vaux-le-Vicomte.

The tradition of China is an entirely different one. It is obviously the mother of the gardens in the vast Chinese territory, and it is the basis of the gardens of Japan and Korea. It backlights the gardens of Asia, possibly even as far south as Bali. We Westerners tend constantly to underestimate its quantitative and qualitative significance, because we speak the garden language of Persia. Superficially we think we see intrinsic similarities, as when modernist architects reduce the Japanese garden to Zen Buddhist asceticism, or when the eighteenth century was so taken with the notion of asymmetry. But the intrinsic difference is great. It is questionable, for example, whether we can speak of an earthly paradise in the Chinese gardening tradition.

Whereas the Western tradition, be it Christian or Islamic, controls nature – with the *genius loci* as its antagonist, a kind of serpent in paradise – such things have no appeal in the Chinese tradition. This tradition *worships* the dragon of the *genius loci*. It subordinates the garden culture to nature. The best approach is to acknowledge the overriding significance of nature. The Chinese tradition restrains human beings rather than nature. Far more than in the West, society and culture are regimented, with town planning and dwellings reflecting Confucian sternness and order. But the garden intervenes here as a different world, where the language of Tao is spoken, the language of deference to the uncontrollable forces of nature.

The garden is consciously seen as a microcosm, the cosmos on a tiny scale. It does not matter whether the microcosm is in a bowl on the table, the miniature landscapes of pen-jing, or bonsai. A small garden effortlessly draws in a nearby mountain top or even a full moon as a borrowed landscape. As I mentioned before, humankind fundamentally surrenders here to the chaotic flow of nature. The Chinese gardening tradition cultivates the transient and temporary nature of human existence.

These gardens speak the language of Chuangtze.[7] He tells of the famous lute player Zhao, who abruptly decided to give up playing when he realized that by playing one sound he disregarded all other sounds. Only by not playing could he hear all things in complete harmony. Unlike human music, only the music of nature is perfect and will never be less than that.

Curiously enough, there is one point where the divergent Western and Eastern gardening traditions overlap. That is in the city garden, the type I was referring to when I spoke about the Dutch and the Venetian *genius loci*. The garden as microcosm is compatible with all sorts of surroundings – a mountain top or an island in a lake. That is why the gardens of the Chinese men of letters, from the literate civil-service estate, could nestle within the walls of family dwellings. As a refuge for harried officials, the city garden offered safety and relaxation. It was the poetry of human existence beside their official prose. It was a *giardino segreto*. Many of the city gardens of Venice and the Dutch cities also serve this function. The Eastern and Western traditions meet at this level.

I believe that in our time harmony with nature is harder and harder to find, while there is a growing need to seek respite from social obligations, from sounds, from human contact. A reappraisal of the city garden would be one solution. Garden books show that this is already a topical issue in some circles. A Western city garden can learn much from examples within its own tradition, such as those of Italy. But it can also learn from the East. In Suchow, inner spaces have been created that allow nature to breathe. Couldn't the city garden be the cradle of a worldwide garden project?

I have discussed the language of the garden in various ways. There are different languages, each of which has something to say about the relationship between man and nature. What language will the garden of the future speak? Undoubtedly the current revival of the art of gardening is fostered by our growing prosperity. Our world is now full of new wealth, our culture is *nouveau riche*. It is in line with this spending pattern that people discover exterior decorating as a natural counterpart to interior decorating. There is nothing wrong with this. One expression of the earthly paradise as I see it is to indulge in the horn of plenty. At the most, one could argue for more refinement and taste in this green exterior decorating – a bit less show and a bit more humility.

But if we listen to gardens as we listen to stories, then today's garden reveals another aspect. The storytellers are not only as rich, they are cosmopolitan, having collected their botanical materials and garden ideas all over the world. With their expansive way of life these modern big spenders are creating new niches for the garden – in airports, golf courses, hotels, city rooftops, shopping malls. But only at the most superficial, ornamental level have they developed a language that can do justice to this abundance. Many such paradises lack their serpents and dragons. Even so, it is already a big improvement that, for a quarter of a century now, garden makers have gone back to working with the *genius loci* and garden traditions without having to feel guilty.

To create a work of art with the language of the garden requires personality. The voice of nature and the human voice have to be in harmony. Such a profound grasp of nature is the privilege of the very few. It is a criterion for great art in gardening. What is needed is spirituality (if I may use that word), and this cannot be bought with money, it cannot be learned as a profession, nor is it even the monopoly of artists. Great gardens have been made by amateurs and monks, heartbroken lovers, mad princes, and school drop-outs. Such spirituality is a talent.

I should like to close with a poem that many have found moving.[8] It is by one of the greatest garden designers known to history, Nur Jahan. It is found on her simple tomb in the garden she had built for her husband Jahangir when she was empress. The themes I have tried to bring forward here all remarkably converge in this poem – the garden, humanity, language, mortality and paradise. At the zenith of their garden culture, the Mughals made the tomb the centrepoint of the garden, which itself was an image of paradise. We know the Taj Mahal. What epitaph did this poet and maecenas, creator of countless earthly paradises, choose for her tomb?

Upon my grave when I shall die,
No lamp shall burn nor jasmin lie,
No candle with unsteady flame
Serve as reminder of my fame;
No bulbul, chanting overhead,
Shall tell the world that I am dead.

Silence about one's own death is perhaps the ultimate profession of faith in life. Human language merges here flawlessly with the language of the garden.

* *This text was read at the opening of the exhibition 'Aardse Paradijzen. De tuin in de Nederlandse kunst. 15de-18de eeuw' (Earthly Paradises. The Garden in Dutch Art. 15th-18th Centuries), at the Frans Hals Museum, Haarlem, on 14 September 1996.*

1 Russell Page, *The Education of a Gardener*, 1983, pp. 45-46.
2 Erik de Jong and Marleen Dominicus-van Soest, *Aardse Paradijzen. De tuin in de Nederlandse kunst. 15de-18de eeuw*, Ghent, 1996, p. 14.
3 Adriaan van der Staay, *Van Parken en Tuinen*, The Hague, 1989.
4 Charles W. Moore, William J. Mitchell and William Turnbull, Jr., *The Poetics of Gardens*, 1989, pp. 13ff.
5 C. M. Villiers-Stuart, *Gardens of the Great Mughals*, New Delhi, 1983, pp. 20ff.
6 Zahiruddin Muhammad Babur, *Le Livre de Babur. Mémoires de Zahiruddin Muhammad Babur de 1494 à 1529*, Paris, 1980, p. 338.
7 Tsai Chih Chung, *The Music of Nature*, Princeton, 1992.
8 S. Crowe and S. Haywood, *The Gardens of Mughul India*, London, 1992, p. 131.

Neercanne: A status quo of history, research and design
FRIDY DUTERLOO

IN 1989 THE OWNER OF Neercanne Castle, Mr. Camille Oostwegel, expressed his wish to restore the baroque terrace garden, as designed for Baron van Dopff between 1700 and 1713. An archaeological field research was therefore undertaken by the Maastricht City Council and the Technical University of Delft, as part of a general architectural research into the history of Maastricht. In 1991, under the auspices of the Foundation Neercanne Castle Gardens, the archaeological survey was followed by a documentary research undertaken by Klazien Brummel, a student from the Department of Architectural History at the Free University of Amsterdam.[1] The aim of the research was to trace the history and the iconography of the garden, focusing on the early-eighteenth-century situation, when the garden was laid out under the ownership of Baron Daniel Wolff van Dopff.

Both the results of the archaeological and documentary research show that the garden of Neercanne Castle is of great historic interest with considerable local and regional significance. Additionally it became clear that the garden, because of its unique situation and its design, has a great national and even international importance. It was generally felt that if the garden was to be restored, more planning and discussion with owners, interested organizations and local authorities were necessary.

Therefore, on 14 December 1994 a study day at Neercanne Castle was held for which delegates of the Dutch State Commission for Monuments, experts in the field of garden conservation and garden historians were invited. The day was organized by the Sub-Committee for Culture of the Netherlands UNESCO Commission and the Foundation Neercanne Castle Gardens. During the several presentations, the owners' proposals for future management and a possible restoration were discussed. Furthermore information was given on the architectural and historical significance of the garden and its surrounding cultural landscape. Also, comparisons were made with gardens in France, and with the historic landscapes of contemporary Dutch country estates. The final discussion, held at the end of the study day, raised many, sometimes conflicting issues, especially concerning the question of how to approach the safeguarding and possible restoration of the Neercanne garden. It became clear

that a restoration of the Neercanne garden would be a complicated but nevertheless important project. The main concern was to what degree the historic remains in the garden should be conserved, restored and/or reconstructed, and if authenticity should be the main aim. It was concluded that a multiplicity of restoration scenarios and management plans was needed to evaluate the various opinions on their own merits.

After the study-day, UNESCO 'adopted' the Neercanne garden as one of its pilot schemes within its wider interregional project 'Les Espaces du Baroque'. With the financial support of UNESCO, an international conference was held in Maastricht in September 1995, with the aim to invite experts in the field of garden history, landscape conservation, architecture and horticulture, to exchange their ideas and knowledge in general and to express their valuable opinions on a possible future restoration plan for the Neercanne garden. The papers read during this conference and the reports from the various workshops are presented in this publication.

1 Map of Canne, measured by Hansen in 1843, scale 1:2500 (detail). Land Registry, Hasselt

2 Neercanne Castle from the air during the building and archaeological research in 1989. (Photo: Technical University of Delft, Department of Restoration)

1 *The Neercanne garden today*

Neercanne Castle lies in the valley of the river Jeker, south of the city of Maastricht, on the Belgium border in the village Canne (figs. 1-2). In 1679 the castle, probably dating back to the early seventeenth century, was bought by Baron Daniel Wolff van Dopff (c. 1655-1718), who, in 1698, made plans for the restoration, the extension of the main buildings, and for the new layout of the grounds. From circa 1700 to 1713 the formal pleasure gardens were laid out on the east side of the castle (fig. 7). The name of a possible architect and/or designer has never been identified.

Today Neercanne Castle and its several outbuildings are used as a restaurant and as a venue for receptions, meetings and conferences. It is built close to the face of a cliff. The east front faces the river valley with extensive views over the hills on the other side. Behind the castle, on the steep cliffs, lies the former 'Sterrebos', a starred wood of which some of the formal path layout, planting and built structures exist above ground (figs. 3 and 4). The drive running from

the Cannerweg at the north side of the castle leads to a parking area used by the visitors of the restaurant. On the east side of the castle, as seen from the Cannerweg, are the remains of the formal garden, laid out in four terraces (figs. 5 to 7). The first terrace can be reached via the castle and is used by the restaurant. The second and the third terrace, both walled, can be reached via the rounded towers on each side in the wall and via central steps. Although this part is open to the guests of the restaurant, it is not used regularly. The third terrace holds the remains, both above and under ground, of a central pond and a geometrical path layout. Today the second and the third terrace are laid out as grass lawns and are grazed by sheep. The sloping hill on the east side of the castle is now used as a vineyard. The fourth terrace was laid out in the valley of the Jeker, on the other side of the Cannerweg. Today this land is in different ownership (the foundation Het Limburgs Landschap [The Limburg Landscape]), and is kept as a nature reserve and destined to be developed as a wet ecological riverside. The remains of the fourth terrace are still to be seen: they contain an oval-shaped natural stone pond, in desperate need of repair and heavily overgrown (fig. 6). Some of the structural planting, such as trees, still exists, mostly dating

4

3 The valley of the Jeker towards the north in the direction of Maastricht, seen from the slope behind the castle. (Photo: Erik de Jong, 1993)

4 Neercanne as approached from the north. (Photo: Erik de Jong, 1993)

from the nineteenth century. There is no evidence above ground of avenues and/or parterres from the earlier formal garden layout.

2 *Neercanne Castle and its main documentary sources*

There are some very good documentary sources giving information on the design and planting of the early-eighteenth-century Neercanne garden. One of the most valuable sources is a description of the garden by F. Halma, published in 1715. It is illustrated with an engraving by Guillaume Le Bruyn, showing the castle with its surrounding pleasure gardens in a bird's-eye view (fig. 7). In his lyrical appraisal, Halma mentions several flowers, plants and fruits that were growing in Van Dopff's garden at Neercanne. In 1710 the grounds of Van Dopff's estate were measured and drawn up. The report and the measured drawing are now kept in Maastricht's Municipal Archive, in the Poswick file number 1. Other information on the history of Neercanne can be found in the family archive of Neercanne Castle, unfortunately largely lost during a fire. The remains of this archive are now held at the State Archive in Maastricht. Furthermore the contemporary papers of the bailiff Johan Overhoff, now held

in Maastricht's Municipal Record Office, give more insight in the architectural history of Neercanne.

That Van Dopff must have been aware of the artistic and architectural taste of the aristocracy of his time, becomes clear in C. Hop's travel diary. He had made, with Van Dopff, a diplomatic visit to Germany in the early eighteenth century. From his descriptions it is clear that they visited, as was fashionable at the time, many estates, courts and pleasure gardens.

In the early eighteenth century Maastricht and its surroundings were strongly influenced by neighbouring Germany and the prosperous Belgium town of Liège. Geographically these regions show many comparisons; the same counts for their art and architecture. It was very common for architects, carpenters and sculptors to work in a neighbouring country. It is therefore not strange that between 1738 and 1744 *Les Délices du Pais de Liège* was published. The book, existing of five volumes, includes a description of the Neercanne Estate and a collection of engravings and descriptions of several other castles and estates, all not far from Neercanne (fig. 8).

Unfortunately, existing contemporary maps do not show much detail of the pleasure gardens. Only a later map of Canne, dating from 1843 and made by Hansen – kept at the Land Registry Office in Hasselt, Belgium – shows the gardens of Neercanne in more detail (see fig. 1).

3 A description of the early-eighteenth-century garden

On the basis of the above-mentioned documentary sources and the evidence found during the archaeological research, it is possible to give a fairly accurate description of the several features of the garden of Neercanne, as laid out between 1700 and 1713 (compare also figs. on pp. 55-59).[2]

THE TERRACED GARDEN   The first terrace, connected with the south façade of the castle, was the so-called *buitenkamer* or 'outdoor room', which functioned as a small private garden and was seen more or less as an extension of the castle itself. Halma describes that there was a small pond with a powerful fountain. He also mentions the extensive views that could be enjoyed from this high terrace. The engraving by Le Bruyn shows parterres with on each corner a small tree clipped in a geometrical shape. The garden wall is an important feature, since it has in each corner two rounded towers with steps leading to the second terrace. This long rectangular terrace had, according to Halma's description, extensive lattice-work attached to the wall, where several varieties of

5 The terraced gardens at Neercanne as seen from the first floor of Neercanne house. (Photo: Erik de Jong, 1993)

6 View towards the terraced garden and the house, from the ruined pond. (Photo: Erik de Jong, 1993)

fruit were growing, such as apricots, peaches, grapes and red and white roses. The engraving (fig. 7) shows two small pavilions in each corner of the garden, which are lined up with the rounded towers of the terrace above. The pavilions on the engravings might also be the two aviaries that are mentioned in the description of Neercanne in *Les Délices du Pais de Liège*. In the report accompanying the measured drawing of 1710, the existence of these two pavilions or aviaries is confirmed again: the terrace is described as having 'pleasure pavilions' standing between the castle and the 'flower beds'.

The third terrace can be reached from the second terrace via the central steps. An invoice of 1715 confirms that the lower walls of the second terrace were extensively decorated with vases and stucco ornaments, such as described by Halma and shown on Le Bruyn's engraving. Other invoices from 1706 and 1715 mention decorative vases for specific plants and trees, as for example laurel and orange trees. It is likely that somewhere at Neercanne there was also an orangery to bring the vases with the small trees inside during the winter months, but this is not mentioned in any of the documents. The third terrace is enclosed by a high wall with three entrances closed off by ornamental gates, one in the east wall, leading to the Cannerweg, and one in the south and the north wall. Halma describes this large terrace more extensively than the other terraces. He describes it as having a 'flower carpet' and therefore must have shown

7

F. Duterloo *Neercanne: A status quo of history, research and design* the main parterre. *Les Délices du Pais de Liège* mentions that the parterre was divided into squares. The engraving shows trees clipped in a pyramid shape, placed on every corner. According to Halma's description, several fruit varieties were growing on the walls, and invoices from 1705-6 mention box hedges. The engraving also shows two statues standing on both sides of the fountain in the centre. Halma does mention the statues, but unfortunately he does not indicate who was depicted. He informs us that the faces of the figures were turned to the fountain, and that they were surrounded by box hedges. The statues as shown on the engraving could be interpreted as the mythological figures Mercury and either Flora or Diana.

During the archaeological survey, the central fountain was found with the small surrounding wall; all in fair condition (fig. 9). The outer lines of the different square-shaped compartments in the parterre were also found. Unfortunately a planting scheme of the parterre, which must have been quite extensive, has not been found.

In 1705 Van Dopff was able to purchase the ground on the other side of the public road (the Cannerweg), where he could design a fourth terrace, to be reached by an ornamental gate aligned on the central axis of the garden. Halma starts his 'tour' of the garden here, following 'Neptune's view up to the castle and the woods behind'. Neptune, as Halma describes, was sitting in the middle

7 Guillaume Le Bruyn. *Perspective of Neercanne and Its Gardens.* Engraving. In F. Halma, *Het kasteel van Aigermont en d'omleggende lantstreeken in de heerlykheit van Nederkan.* Leeuwarden, 1715. (Photo: University Library, Amsterdam)

8 *The Castle of Hamal (near Tongeren).* Engraving. In R. Le Loup, *Les Délices du Pais de Liège et de la Comté de Namur.* Vol. I, part 1. Liège, 1738-44

of the large oval-shaped pond on a dolphin, and was holding a trident in his right hand. The statue was surrounded by water jets. That Halma's description must have been accurate is shown by documents informing that works were carried out on the dolphin in the large pond in August 1712 and May 1715. In the pond, as depicted on the engraving, there was a small boat. An invoice of 1708 tells us that repairs were carried out on this boat by a local carpenter. During the archaeological survey, the remains of eight steps leading to the pond were found; they could either have functioned as a cascade or indeed as steps to reach a boat.

Halma also describes a series of long avenues on the fourth terrace as shown on the engraving and he mentions the existence of lime-trees and hedges. There is no documentary evidence on the further layout and planting of the fourth terrace, except for the engraving and the remains found during the archaeological research. The east side of the pond was probably closed off by a semicircular-shaped flower bed, and the whole terrace was surrounded by hedges and wooden fences, as is shown on the engraving.

THE 'STERREBOS' OR STARRED WOOD   The wood, called the 'Sterrebos', on the hills behind the castle, shown on the engraving with its long avenues laid out in the shape of a star, is intriguing. In reality this area is very steep and the avenues must have been running either up- or downhill, as is described by Halma. He mentions the several tree species to be found in the wood, such as elms, beeches and alders.

The engraving shows a small pavilion, probably a belvedere, from which one could enjoy extensive views over the garden and the Jeker valley. In 1710, 224 'small windows of fine glass' were bought for it. During his journey up the hill, Halma reports that he found a water reservoir with a pump from which the fountains and other water features in the garden were managed. Documentary evidence shows that the pump was indeed installed in 1707. An invoice of 1715 tells us that small lead and copper pipes were bought for the fountain-heads. Many other invoices have been found describing works that were undertaken in the wood, such as sweeping the avenues and planting hedges along them. The design and planting of the wood must have taken a long time; in 1714 another ten days were spent on the layout of a long avenue.

It is likely that statues were placed in the wood, since one invoice mentions the work on a 'Hercules'. The engraving by Le Bruyn shows also an obelisk, in the centre, and an amphitheatre, situated between the castle and the wood. Neither of them is mentioned in any of the documentary sources. It is likely that where the avenues came together in the centre there would have been a sculpture of some kind. An amphitheatre is also a feature seen very often in baroque formal gardens, influenced by the Italian Renaissance gardens. The cliff behind the castle could have been an ideal spot for an open-air theatre and it is known that Van Dopff was a great admirer of theatre and drama. Today, south of the castle in the cliffs, one can still see a semicircular man-made coomb or hollow, although it is not certain what its function was.

ICONOGRAPHICAL THEMES AND INFLUENCE OF THE LANDSCAPE It is important to remember that it was the wider surrounding landscape that formed the main backdrop for the garden and the castle. The surrounding landscape that belonged to the estate was used for agricultural purposes and included orchards and vineyards. Halma mentions that there were extensive orchards on both sides of the castle, and he describes them as 'Pomona's gifts'. According to the description in *Les Délices du Pais de Liège*, there was also a vegetable garden and a walled area where small wild animals were kept. It can be concluded that the estate not only functioned as an ideal country house outside the busy town, but that it was after all also functioning as a farm, which cultivated vegetables and fruits and kept cattle.

9 The excavated fountain on the third terrace, former centre of the parterre. (Photo: Erik de Jong, 1993)

Like in most other early-eighteenth-century formal gardens, the terrace garden of Neercanne Castle must have had an iconographical scheme, as is shown by Halma's descriptions and Le Bruyn's engraving. It must have centred on Van Dopff's military career (the bastion-like character of the terraced garden, palms as decoration above the entrance in the west front and on the ceiling in the hall) and the bounties of nature (for example, the vines and grapes sculptured on the garden front). As mentioned above, there were several statues, fountains and pavilions placed in the garden referring to classical and mythological figures. Like most other Dutch seventeenth-century gardens, the Neercanne garden and its features must have functioned and must have been experienced as a symbol for Van Dopff's position in society, reflecting his political position and ideas as well as his perception of country life.

4 *A future for the garden of Neercanne*

It can be concluded that although the planted components of the Neercanne garden have mainly disappeared or are in poor condition, the general early-eighteenth-century design of the garden – such as land form, water features and built structures – has survived, though in some cases needs repairing or consolidating. A detailed and authentic restoration or reconstruction of the planted components could recover the designed effects, and could consolidate the degree of survival. However, in the case of Neercanne, where the documentary sources such as planting schemes are almost non-existent, it might be preferable to opt for a conservation and management plan that safeguards and reflects the essence of the original design, instead of choosing for a scenario that opts for a reconstruction or restoration 'in spirit'.

The castle, its outbuildings, the garden walls and the terraces, with their historical layers as they appear today, are very important components of the garden, and should not be ignored in the conservation plan. These remains of the so-called 'hard landscaping' should be seen as the structural focal points which give us the main layout of the garden. Choosing and planting fruit and flower varieties as mentioned by Halma could support the overall effect of a convincing and non-intrusive restoration.

Like the castle, the garden, with its planting, has also several historic layers, of which the early-eighteenth-century layout seems the most dominant – though further research on the different historic layers of the garden might indicate that these are historically equally important and interesting. There exists, for example, a daguerreotype of 1844 showing the large oval pond, the walls and terraces, but with quite a different planting scheme, which has partly survived (see fig. on p. 30). In a future conservation plan this historical layer should not be ignored.

The fact that the garden is currently in divided ownership will inevitably have its influences on its future management. As already mentioned, the fourth terrace with the remains of the large oval-shaped pond is currently owned by the foundation Het Limburgs Landschap. Their wish is to maintain the site as a naturally and ecologically balanced landscape, with the river Jeker forming the main basis for a rich plantlife and the attraction of wildlife. A thorough restoration or reconstruction of the formal garden would, from their point of view, not be compatible with their own thoughts on the future of the landscape.

On the other hand, the owner of the castle, with the restaurant and the larger part of the garden, has expressed his wish to restore and/or reconstruct the garden to its early-eighteenth-century formal design. In the future he would like to open the gardens both to the guests of his restaurant and to the general public. Such a future restoration scheme would have to take into account an increase of visitor numbers, and demanding parking facilities, etc. It may be difficult in finding a fine balance between on the one hand the safeguarding of a historic garden of great interest, and on the other hand running the garden as a possible tourist attraction.

The issues described above are only a few of the ones discussed in the papers and workshop reports presented at the conference, as published in this book. All presentations contain many ideas, philosophies, practical solutions and critical notes on garden and landscape conservation in general and specifically on the future plans for Neercanne, regardless of the 'restoration scenario' that will be chosen in the future. It will therefore be a valuable source of information and discussion for everybody in the field of garden and landscape conservation, history of gardens, architecture and horticulture.

---

1 K. Brummel, '«Natuur met kunst vereent»; historisch onderzoek naar de vroeg 18e-eeuwse situatie van de terrastuin van Kasteel Neercanne', in *Bulletin KNOB*, 92 (1993), 4, pp. 89-113.
2 Ibid. The description given in this paragraph is based on the descriptions and interpretations of the Neercanne garden given by Klazien Brummel in her article, '«Natuur met kunst vereent»', a research resulting from a collaboration between the Technical University of Delft, Monumentenzorg Maastricht and the Architectural History Department of the Free University of Amsterdam.

Neercanne Castle and the Dutch garden tradition

ERIK DE JONG

LANDSCAPE AND DESIGN In 1995 in the Netherlands, we commemorated the death of Jac. P. Thijsse (1861-1945), well-known Dutch nature conservationist, initiator and founding father of our national parks and nature reserves, advocate of the study and protection of wild and indigenous Dutch plants.[1] Much of our present-day concepts of Dutch landscape is based on his ideas about the specific character of Dutch nature and flora – ideas which were widely propagated by the small pictures that could be collected and pasted in the famous Verkade albums, devoted to 'the dunes', 'spring' and the like. Those ideas not only created a common image of Dutch landscape as 'natural' in its emphasis on flora and fauna, types of soil, biotopes and geography, they also extended to the field of garden and park design. The planting of Thijsse's Hof in Bloemendaal, for example, carried out together with the landscape architect Springer in the 1920s, shows his ideal of a landscape in a park, where different families of plants are brought together to exemplify different types of Dutch landscape, such as the dunes along the coast. More extensively, his ideas on national plants were used in the so-called *heem* parks, of which the Thijsse Park of the late 1930s in Amstelveen (south of Amsterdam) is the most beautiful, showing how with great investments an artistic form of wild and indigenous nature could be created.[2]

In Thijsse's legacy, Dutch landscapes and parks were once and for all brought into the realm of free nature as opposed to the artificiality of culture: designed nature represented artificiality itself. It is, broadly speaking, this contrast between nature and culture which persists to this very day, when the emphasis on the ecological aspects of nature development may be seen as a second blossoming of the tradition created by Thijsse earlier this century. Increasing natural and ecological values has priority in current landscape politics and is stimulated by many institutions, first of all by the Dutch Government with its Ecological Main Structure for the Netherlands of 1990; one might even

1 Neercanne in an early daguerreotype of 1844. As usual with a daguerreotype, the object is represented in mirror image. Municipal Archives, Historical Topographical Atlas, Maastricht, no. 2609

say that the gist of the current debate on the future of Dutch landscape is the antithesis between nature by ecology and nature by design.[3]

At the same time, the general public no longer seemed to realize that much of the Dutch landscape, including polders, forests, agricultural land, parks and gardens, was indeed created by design. During the 1950s, in particular, parks became part of urbanistic and architectonic design; the design of gardens mostly remained hidden and unnoticed in the private sector, while landscape was either protected because of its natural values – thus becoming a metaphor of true nature in general – or redesigned to meet new economic demands, and so became a symbol of 'unnatural' landscape. Gradually, during the past fifteen years, it became clear to some of us that the Dutch landscape is pre-eminently an artificial and cultural landscape, in the sense that it was not only shaped by man for many purposes, but also moulded by his expectations, imagination, projections, love and illusions with regard to nature and landscape. Slowly, the insight is growing that designed nature does not have to mean that nature is excluded at the cost of traditional naturalness or modern ecology. We even begin to see that Dutch culture has quite a tradition in designing nature past and present, backed by long-standing traditions in botany, horticulture and design. The report on cultural landscape published by the Ministry of Culture in 1994 actualizes in a most fascinating way the significance of landscape and culture as mutually inspiring and supporting constants in Dutch society.[4]

2

Nevertheless, by many the geometry of a formal garden is still seen as the opposite to a natural landscape. If, however, we would interpret this opposition in the sense of contrast, we might detect values that for long have escaped our attention. The gardens and the house of Neercanne in the Jeker valley, which were the topic of the discussions during the UNESCO conference, may prove that both geometrical garden and landscape form an integral part of a cultural landscape and that both are in many ways related as a product of man's culture in his ever-changing relationship with nature.

IMAGES OF THE GARDEN   In Guillaume Le Bruyn's engraving of a bird's-eye view of Neercanne castle, published as an illustration to Halma's poem of 1715, the complex of house and gardens looks admirably clear and detailed (see fig. on p. 24).[5] Being the only contemporary sources, both the poetic description and the crisp bird's-eye view are most likely to be considered prime sources for restoration. Apparently, their appeal is stronger than the later history of the castle and its gardens, as shown in a very early and rare daguerreotype of 1844, where walls and terraces are grown over with vegetation (fig. 1) and the large pond is still filled with water – an image confirmed by other topographical drawings from that period and from this century.[6]

These two images, separated by a span of about 230 years, confront us with the way we look at the present situation of the gardens and the house at Neer-

2 Aerial photograph of Neercanne Castle, its gardens and surrounding landscape, in 1983. Topographical Service, Emmen

3 Philippe van Gulpen. *View of the Façade and Terraces of the Castle of Neercanne, from the East.* c. 1848. Pen in grey-brown, washed with colour. Municipal Archives, Historical Topographical Atlas, Collection Van der Noordaa, Maastricht, no. 455

canne, another 150 years later. Both engraving and daguerreotype show situations which may be termed 'authentic': the engraving, if it is to be believed, referring to a then recent garden, crisp and clear, the daguerreotype showing an aged garden and house, where parts have been altered and added to, yet, in its partial decay, producing an atmospheric richness.

The fact that excavations on the now derelict terraces have yielded information on the garden at its zenith around 1710 seems to make the engraving a more valuable and attractive source than the daguerreotype. The engraving has thus become a pretext for a tendency to value the early-eighteenth-century situation higher than the situation in 1844. We must keep in mind, though, that Le Bruyn's engraving was never intended to play such a role. He manipulated the perspective so as to show terraced gardens in front and at both sides of the house, together with the Sterrebos. To this end, he devised what became almost a second main axis running through the avenue in front of the picture plane towards the amphitheatre and the centre of the Sterrebos. A closer look shows that the difference in elevation between river and castle is almost completely ignored. A comparison with the information from the excavations proves that the proportions in the engraving are larger than life. Also, most of the details do not correspond with what is known from other sources, such as (later) maps and archival records. A case in point are the three straight avenues in the lower garden: did they really exist, and if so, where did they lead to? An aerial photograph does seem to show traces of them, although this information has not been substantiated by archaeological or other research (fig. 2).

4

We must conclude that, on the whole, the engraving has less informative value than was at first realized: it does not depict reality. On the other hand, it still is an interesting source for the historian, even though, like many other engravings from this period, its value is largely propagandistic – as is that of its counterpart, the poem.[7] Besides, the precise lines of the engraver's technique suggest a clear and detailed layout, which never existed. Indeed, also in the garden style around 1700 plant material softened and enlivened the more formal lines of the design. In that respect, the daguerreotype shows a much livelier picture of the gardens, where the straight walls are in contrast with the free forms of nature.

Caution, therefore, is required in our approach to Neercanne: from the start, we must be aware of our intentions, our wishes and our interpretations of the different historical and archaeological sources available, especially if not even all data have been gathered. There is the paradox that by our own attitude we could destroy more authentic material than we could gain by our wish to reconstruct an 'authentic' early-eighteenth-century garden. Why indeed should we want to restore, or, in the case of Neercanne, reconstruct? There is a curious parallel with the way Philippe van Gulpen drew Neercanne in 1848 (fig. 3), only four years after the daguerreotype, showing the third terrace and the pond cleaned of debris, as if an early love of history long before our time already tried to reconstruct Neercanne to a former architectural elegance. From other angles as well, the terraces at Neercanne were popular with nineteenth-century topographers and antiquarians (fig. 4).

5

4 Alexander Schaepkens. *Detail of the Stairs on the Third Terrace at Neercanne, seen from the North-East.* c. 1850. Pencil, washed with green and white. Municipal Archives, Historical Topographical Atlas, Maastricht, no. 1688

5 View from the second terrace at Neercanne towards the third terrace, the northern terraces with their fruit-trees, and the valley. (Photo: Erik de Jong, 1993)

It is not since long that the Dutch garden of the seventeenth and early eighteenth centuries is seen as a valuable and important part of Dutch culture and that it has a specific story to tell in a West European context. A steady growth of garden history as an independent discipline during the past fifteen years has certainly contributed to the recognition of the value of gardens, old and new. Other factors, such as the approaching end of the life cycle of many older parks, a generally 'greener' consciousness and the sudden emancipation of modern garden and park design reflecting its own history, have all led to the recognition of the value of parks and gardens and their tradition.

The effect of the reconstruction of the gardens of Het Loo, completed eleven years ago, should not be underestimated. This first large-scale interpretation of a late-seventeenth-century Dutch garden confronted both experts and visitors with a spatial layout, a novel use of plantings, water and decoration, which formed a contrast with what was generally seen as nature inside and outside the garden.

The positive side of the reconstruction of Het Loo is the attempt to re-create an 'authentic' planting of parterres with their *plates-bandes* in a clearly defined spatial layout. The negative point is that the garden was conceived almost as an autonomous work of art, with no relation whatever to its surroundings – a situation which did not correspond with its original intent. The vast sums invested have resulted in the Loo gardens being confined to their inwardly oriented composition. Many details of this reconstruction were dictated, among other things, by the wealth of engravings used for it, although these had never been checked for their reliability as a source. On the basis of this contemporary material and supported by a then prevailing opinion to look

6

upon the late-seventeenth-century style of Dutch gardens as 'French', the reconstruction of Het Loo has been forced into an ideal image of a Dutch garden 'in the French style'. Het Loo, of course, was a unique project, and it can hardly be a good example for Neercanne, even though they are related through Neercanne's founder Daniel Wolff van Dopff, military governor of Maastricht and as such connected with the court circles of Stadholder-King William III.

A PLACE IN GARDEN HISTORY   What is the meaning of the Neercanne gardens in the light of Dutch garden history? If we undertake a reconstruction or restoration, we must first assess their historical significance.

Van Dopff (c.1655-1718), military governor of Maastricht, bought the manor of Neercanne in 1679, with rights and privileges. The occupation of Maastricht by the French troops in 1673 had ravaged the countryside surrounding the city as well as the Jeker valley: it enabled Van Dopff to re-create a whole new house with gardens. From 1699 to 1710 most of the complex must have been completed and it is very likely that house and gardens were designed according to a unified geometrical plan. Possibly Van Dopff himself was responsible for a large part of the design, which was not uncommon in his time

6 The plantation of fruit-trees on the northern terraces at Neercanne. (Photo: Erik de Jong, 1993)
7 The vineyard at Neercanne on the slope, south of the house and the terraces. (Photo: Erik de Jong, 1993)

when many high officials were expert 'amateurs' in the field of gardening and garden layout.[8]

Van Dopff's keen eye must have recognized the advantages of the situation in the Jeker valley: magnificent views led the eye from the slopes of the Canne mountain to fertile and prosperous meadows, a lively stream, Maastricht to the north and the small village of Canne to the south, linked by an almost 'ceremonial' road (see fig. on p. 56). It was a rare situation in the landscape of the Dutch Republic, yet not exceptional in the southern part of the province of Limburg and the region around Liège, now Belgium. It is the views which must have meant a lot to Van Dopff personally, because looking round, he could see some of the main scenes of his life: the fortifications of Maastricht and the fort of St. Peter which he designed himself, both reminding him of towns and war, both typical of his professional activities. Seen in the light of the war with France, the battles fought around Maastricht in 1673 took on symbolic significance in the power politics pursued by William III. And not only for him, but also for his opponent Louis XIV, Maastricht marked a stage in their aggressive warfare: the seizing of Maastricht by the French is proudly commemorated in the Galerie des Glaces at Versailles, which was executed from 1678 to 1686 by Le Brun. In 1700, however, after the peace with France by the Treaty of Rijswijk (1698), Van Dopff could enjoy the view of his own gardens into a green valley, where agricultural activities took place and viniculture and fruit farming were being developed, symbolizing a peaceful, Virgilian country life which had been restored after the war.

From the records it appears that Van Dopff went to great pains to take possession of the pastures between the road and the river. Up to 1705 he gradually acquired more land, thus transforming the natural landscape into a cultural landscape where agriculture, viniculture, fruit farming and roads and meadows lined with trees determined its essential quality (figs. 5, 6 and 7). In many ways, the gardens and the house were the apotheosis of this whole, pearls in a splendid crown, showing that from agriculture to gardening it was only a few delicate steps (fig. 8). If documents and the descriptions of the poem are to be believed, much of the gardens on the terraces, including the heavy monumental fortified walls, were planted and grown with peach, pear, apricot and nut-trees, together with laurel and white and red roses, thus mixing the pleasing with the useful into the (economic) essence of a country estate.

In this sense, Van Dopff created a cultural landscape of the first order. It is not without a touch of propaganda that Halma, in his country-house poem, not only celebrated the garden, but also the surrounding landscape – a landscape that in many respects still possesses the above qualities, be it somehow like a Sleeping Beauty to be kissed to life. And I believe that in this slumbering state, Neercanne is unique in the Netherlands.

CLEVES AS A PROTOTYPE OF NEERCANNE   In his personal endeavours to create a landscape with a garden, Van Dopff must have been aware of what the local geography around Maastricht traditionally offered as possibilities for gardens; he must also have been sensitive to what his contemporaries had done before him, or were doing at the same time, since gardens for his generation had become exclusive properties and were much desired as part of one's social status. Not only in his own region there was an interest in forestry, agriculture and horticulture as essential elements of country life. Viniculture, for example, was

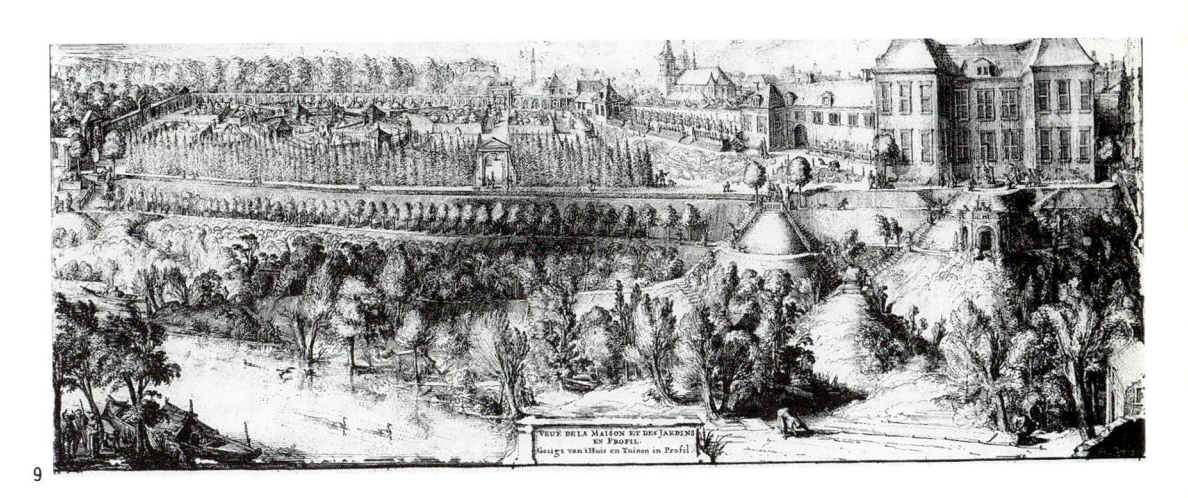

8 The complex of Neercanne Castle from the south-east. (Photo: Erik de Jong, 1993)

9 Romeyn de Hooghe. *The Prince's Garden at Cleves with its Parterres and Terraces, partly designed with a 'wild' garden.* c.1685. Etching. (Photo: Vrije Universiteit, Amsterdam)

almost an impossibility in the Dutch Republic, due to location and climate, yet its classic connotations led several Dutch amateurs to experiment with growing grapes in places where one would least expect them, as in the gardens of Gunterstein in the flat polder landscape along the river Vecht.[9]

As a young man, Van Dopff was trained in Cleves at the court of Johan Maurits van Nassau (1604-1679), famous for his patronage of the arts and an avid creator of gardens and landscapes – not only at Cleves, but also as adviser to the Kurfürst of Brandenburg who, at Van Nassau's instigation, began beautifying the landscape around Potsdam with gardens, orchards, avenues lined with trees, and agricultural land (since 1990 a UNESCO World Heritage Site).[10]

Appointed fort-builder and architect, Van Dopff must have learned to recognize the beauty of the gardens at Cleves, which therefore should be seen as the true prototype of what was later to be realized at Neercanne. Expertly trained as a military man in the essentials of topography, and aware of the close relationship between fortifications and plantings, he was privileged to appreciate quickly how nature's geography could be enhanced with splendid terraced gardens giving magnificent views (figs. 9 and 10). Nor will it have escaped him that Johan Maurits had decorated the gardens with statues, such as a Minerva, a Sleeping Mars and Cupids, and with parterres, fountains, grottoes and buildings, thus dedicating the garden to peace where the arts flowered and Mars was put to rest after the Eighty-Year War ended in 1648.[11] Cleves, Johan

10

Maurits van Nassau's masterpiece, must have taught Van Dopff to value the importance and beauty of a natural site, to appreciate a row of trees lining a street, to absorb a view, to undergo the beauty and usefulness of plants and fruit-trees, giving him insight into the effect of horticulture where human art trains nature to its best results. Most remarkable at Cleves was Johan Maurits' design for a hanging 'wild' garden on the terrace below the parterre garden next to the Prinsenhof, thus creating an intermediary between the geometry of the garden and the wider landscape beyond (fig. 9). These terraces offered possibilities to enjoy the beauties of nature, with, as one of the engravings show, telescopes or large, polished 'Claude glasses' (fig. 10).[12]

That these lessons were not lost on Van Dopff is shown by a diary which records a journey to Vienna through the German countries in 1707, in the company of the young Cornelis Hop, who acted as his secretary. This exploratory trip to these countries may be explained by the fact that Van Dopff was born in Frankfurt, and it sheds an interesting light on mutual cultural influences in the field of gardens and horticulture, the more so since nowadays Dutch gardens from Van Dopff's time are often still seen exclusively from the perspective of contemporary French gardening.[13] It is interesting to read how Van Dopff and his companions comment on gardens in Darmstadt and especially on the panoramas that were created there; they describe the famous terraced gardens of the Hortus Palatinus in Heidelberg and admire them for their situation on the

10 Romeyn de Hooghe. *View from the Terraces below the Prince's Garden at Cleves, with a view towards the Kermis Valley.* c. 1685. Etching. (Photo: Vrije Universiteit, Amsterdam)

11 Perelle. *Part of the Terraced Gardens at Saint-Cloud.* 1670-80. Engraving. Bibliothèque Nationale, Paris

mountain slope with views towards the beautiful river Neckar. They also comment on gardens in Stuttgart which are ill-kept, and record how the conservatory there is stacked with the most beautiful orange and lemon trees. Time and again they compare what they see with how it is done back home in Holland, immediately noticing if trees are planted the 'Dutch' way or if a garden resembles 'our Dutch gardens'. In Vienna, Van Dopff admires the situation of the gardens of the Favorita with its beautiful view on the city; there he also wishes to visit the galleries, terraces and gardens of the famous Neugebäude, but is refused admittance (see fig. on p. 122).

Van Dopff emerges from this diary as a keen amateur with an eye for the various beauties of nature; at the same time, it shows that the interest in designing gardens in relation to land- and cityscapes was international. The military governor must have congratulated himself for owning such a fine terraced garden himself, realizing that elsewhere in the Netherlands he was envied such a well-situated property. Fostered by his experiences at Cleves as a young man and inspired by the stylish gardens in the country of his origin, guided by the circles of the stadholder he served and led by his ambitions as a governor of Maastricht, Van Dopff followed his personal taste and moulded local geography and local traditions into a modern, fashionable landscape. In its perfect blend of nature with art, of the useful with the beautiful, his vision was to emulate, so Halma writes in his poem, all that was done before.

Wasn't a terraced garden full of magic? It evoked the ancient 'hanging gardens' of Babylon, well known in the seventeenth century as the origin of gardening; it also reminded one of the much admired Italian gardens around Florence or Rome, reminiscent of ancient Roman gardens and their descriptions in the letters of, for example, the younger Pliny. It was a tradition not inappropriate for the region around Maastricht, where Romans were known to have settled.[14] More recently, terraced gardens were said to be the personal pride of Louis the XIV. We know that even William III was keenly interested in these garden projects of his antagonist, instructing his favourite Hans Willem Bentinck to report on the gardens of Marly during his ambassadorship at Versailles in 1698. He received a letter in which Bentinck described Marly as 'le plus agreable jardin que j'aye vue et qui plairoit fort à V. Mjté'. To him, it surpassed Versailles, as did Saint-Cloud and Meudon (fig. 11), both envied by the Dutch because of their natural situations. We know from letters that William III, when first planning Het Loo in about 1683, had at first envisaged a situation on one of the hills near Hoog Soeren, which would have given him the views he desired and found appropriate for a trianon-like *maison de chasse* – a scheme abandoned because of the costs involved in leading water to fountains at such a high site.[15]

What the stadholder himself could not achieve, Van Dopff did. Like the garden at Cleves, Neercanne in its cultural landscape offers a garden not often encountered in Dutch history; it provides a rare *trait d'union* between the much admired ancient and modern hillside gardens and a love of gardens at the stadholder's court in the latter half of the seventeenth century.

REVIVING HISTORY   We may assess the uniqueness of Neercanne and its gardens from a historical point of view: for a historian there is always much to be informed about – but restoration is another matter.

Since there is a tendency to evaluate the situation around 1700, it is a great pity that our information on the gardens of Neercanne is so dramatically poor. The archives, the poem, the archaeological excavations have not yielded enough material to give us a clear picture of how the gardens really looked, nor enough insight to bring them back to life. Authenticity then becomes very problematic: a restoration becomes a reconstruction, based on hypotheses.

For any restoration and/or reconstruction it is of vital importance to decide beforehand which direction we wish to take: do we strive for total or partial restoration, for a detailed reconstruction or a simpler solution emphasizing the outlines of the composition, or are we thinking of an altogether modern design? How indeed are we to define the degree of improvement of the present state when we know that the terraces now belonging to the house were once part of a much larger estate, including terraces towards the north, a Sterrebos up on the hill and agricultural land in the Jeker valley?

Each solution had its pros and cons, so it was decided that, before embarking on such a project, the parameters should be defined by a group of international experts.

We need to know, for example, if the design of the garden was based on a solid geometric system, as was usual in Van Dopff's time. From the extant material we may conclude that a geometric design along a main axis determined the layout of the garden behind the house, down the terraces towards the large pond set in the Jeker valley. More specific analysis may help us to determine the architecture of the gardens. It may also help us to understand the place of the geometric plan in the landscape setting. From other examples we know that geometry was used as a means to control and understand nature – in the Dutch Republic it was used to lay out the landscape of the polders, such as the Beemster early in the seventeenth century, and larger and smaller gardens alike.[16] At the same time, these geometric systems referred to the laws governing ideal nature: geometry itself expressed the harmony intrinsic to creation. Art and nature were balanced in an intricate relationship, art helping imperfect nature to strive towards its own perfection, nature finding in geometry a way to express itself to the fullest. That such seventeenth-century concepts matter, and that it is vital to trace them on the site of the garden itself so as to understand what they mean by way of design, becomes apparent from the garden façade at Versailles: there statues of Art and Nature dominate the central projection. They are the guiding forces in any seventeenth- or eighteenth-century garden, responding sensitively to the site's topography, which is always unique and never the same:

the geometric garden contains a great deal of poetry and magic when it comes to defining a harmonious relationship between nature, landscape and design.[17]

Also of vital importance to our problem is the archaeological evidence: where archival and iconographic material is lacking, this evidence may yield not only sound information, but also authentic material (see fig. on p. 19). On the large third terrace, for example, paths were discovered as well as the central basin of the fountain.[18] But here, too, questions arise: is it possible to have archaeological evidence define the physical elements and structures of the garden above, in and under the soil? And to what extent are restoration and presentation of the findings necessary if we want to create an authentic reconstruction, while at the same time we should protect the archive of the soil? What does archaeology yield in terms of botanical evidence; should we excavate the whole site in order to have the possibility to use every detail, every fragment that otherwise might be lost?

THE IMPORTANCE OF DETAILS   The broad outlines of the architecture and the composition of the Neercanne gardens are not difficult to define. The greatest problem of all is how to fill in the structure with the details of planting and ornamentation. Of these, nothing has survived or been found. How are we to reconstruct, for example, the parterre's broderie without exact detailed evidence? In many ways, it represented the most refined art form of nature

12

available – and we are reminded of the words of that famous English gardener and antiquarian, John Evelyn, who in 1686 wrote that in Holland 'Gardens are there so universally affected that their Veneration of Flora and the parterre is extraordinary, and though the French at present may boast of their vast design, their Versailles and portentous works, Gardens can no where be so spruce and accurately kept....'[19]

Would it be possible to reconstruct a convincing historical image of such a parterre, without becoming superficial – and to which local or national examples from the period should we turn? To the parterre at Clingendaal from the 1670s to the 1690s, which is so much similar in form and layout?[20] Which plants and trees should we choose from the scanty evidence left to us in the archives – how should we define height, texture and colour, demanding neither too little nor too much? How take into account the future development of the garden, change being the essence of nature – could we forestall problems by well-defined long-term maintenance? And what about the lost statues and urns mentioned in Halma's poem and only vaguely indicated in the engraving? Should sculptures be brought back, or left out because authenticity is not served by originals which are not in accordance with the historical (and unknown) iconography – or, for that matter, by replicas?

Do we indeed want a historical image, or are we inclined, faced with so many problems, to design along more modern lines, introducing forms and images of our own time, thus protecting the archive in the soil?

13

12 The parterre at Hex Castle.
    (Photo: Erik de Jong, 1995)

13 Terrace at Hex Castle looking towards the vegetable garden.
    (Photo: Erik de Jong, 1995)

All of these problems are there to be discussed during the workshops, by listening to expertise from elsewhere and by visiting the gardens at Hex Castle. Solutions will perhaps be offered, but also criticisms and warnings voiced: there are many examples of good intentions which have resulted in rather pathetic gardens, such as those in Alden Biesen in Belgium, not far from Maastricht.[21]

It is on the basis of these criticisms that plans will have to be developed – the most difficult thing of all being how to realize a suggested solution – to bring back the life and atmosphere of gardens that have been kept with love and care over the years, such as the terraced gardens of Hex (figs. 12 and 13). Created later in the eighteenth century, these gardens stem from a regional tradition around Liège that also influenced Neercanne, which is part of it. At Hex there still is an atmosphere of authenticity, which one also senses in the daguerreotype of Neercanne from 1844.

A GARDEN IN A LANDSCAPE   I have left the most important question for the end. It touches on the vital problem with which this text began: the definition of the relationship between garden and landscape. Should the scanty documentation on the unique site of Neercanne lead us to consider the garden as an autonomous work of art, thereby referring ourselves for lack of informa-

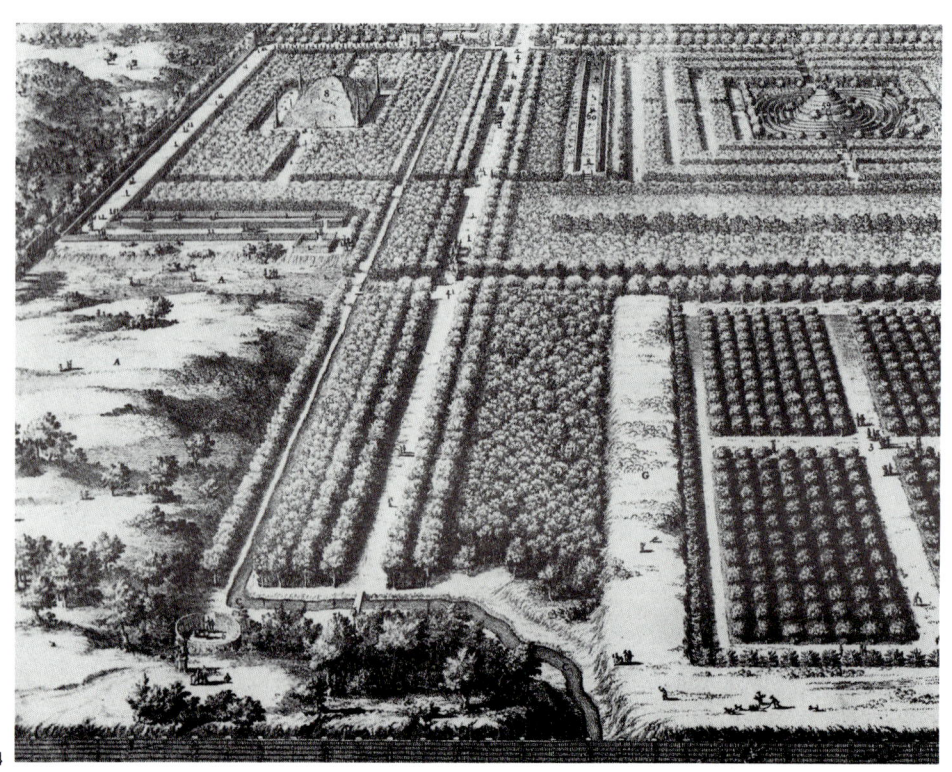

14

tion to comparable details of contemporary gardens in the Maastricht-Liège region, or at the stadholder's court? Or should we try to re-establish a harmonious relationship with the landscape as a whole, a relationship intended by its former owner, of which there are many contemporary examples such as the gardens of Zeist in central Holland and De Voorst in the east, with their long avenues stretching out into the landscape, or smaller gardens such as De Werve near The Hague in the west, where the garden was defined by the parcelling out of the land? There is hardly a garden of this period which, one way or another, was not intricately woven into its landscape setting. Should we detail the gardens to perfection and ignore the quality of the landscape it looks out upon, or try instead to emphasize the qualities of a cultural landscape with a garden?

Meanwhile, we should not forget that the Jeker valley is as unique as the terraced gardens, since little has changed there through the years in the road system, the fields and the course of the stream; also its agricultural function is still there and could be brought out more to advantage. Doesn't the landscape of the valley, with its characteristic silhouette, its meandering river, its flat pastures and its impressive plantations of poplars in straight formal lines, embody a natural architectural order, forming, as it were, a theatre of nature and culture, thus teaching us a lesson in design principles which is repeated in a more refined way in the layout and the design of the castle with its terraced gardens?

14 J. van Avelen. *Bird's-Eye View of the Gardens of Zorgvliet.* Detail showing the south-western part of the plantations where the avenues and the winding brook meet with the 'wild' landscape of the dunes. 1692-98. Engraving. (Photo: Institute for Art History, Utrecht)

15 The orchard next to the main avenue at Eysden Castle. (Photo: Erik de Jong, 1995)

The terraces towards the north (though now part of a nature reserve and not a domain of the garden proper) still have some of the fruit-trees characteristic of the region, and they might be used to bring back this important element, which still functions near other castles in Limburg, such as Eysden Castle, former centre of fruit cultivation (fig. 15).[22] It would reflect the seventeenth-century interest in the cultivation of trees as an essential part of garden culture. This goes for other gardens too, such as Bentinck's Zorgvliet near The Hague, created in 1670-90, where what I would call 'the cult of the tree' reached its peak. Zorgvliet, in fact, is a most interesting garden (fig. 14). On Johan Maurits van Nassau-Siegen's advice of 1674, and following his earlier experiments with the wild garden at Cleves, the lively, natural course of the winding stream was maintained to let it compete with the straight lines of avenues and parterres – which shows that such contrasts were truly appreciated in Van Dopff's own time.[23]

At Neercanne, the union of landscape and garden presents a problem which is difficult to solve because of the divided ownership of the house and terraces on the one hand and the fields across the road, where the remains of the large pond are to be found, on the other. Our modern attitude towards nature only enlarges the division between garden and landscape. To many people, the formality of the once architecturally laid-out terraces not only conflicts with the landscape, its so-called 'artificiality' is also considered to be unnatural. A possible reconstruction of the large pond and perhaps the avenues is to many (the foundation Het Limburgs Landschap, for example) an unacceptable intrusion of the ecology of the natural landscape. One may feel sympathy for this point of view. One would wish for a thorough study of the historical development of this landscape, as much as one wishes it with respect to the garden.

Yet, if we want to treat garden and landscape again as an entity, we will have to find a common denominator to create harmony between these cultural and natural values. The landscape of the Jeker valley is originally and *de facto* a cultural landscape, where man has left his imprint, just as he did in the treatment of the garden. As a cultural landscape, it showed different gradations of nature developing into art, gradations that still exist, though not in the same proportions as those from around 1700. Couldn't these gradations again be used as a starting-point for a restricted architectural treatment of the first three terraces and a simple restoration of the pond on the fourth terrace, at the same time leaving room for the enhancement of the natural 'wild' richness along the river? Couldn't the pastures in the valley be extensively treated, while the river Jeker is developed as an ecological 'wet' site, reintroducing a more 'cultural' natural richness by replanting trees along the road and fruit-trees on the northern terraces? The latter suggestion may find support with the activities of the Foundation for the Preservation of Small Landscape Elements in Roermond, which advocates such an enrichment of the Limburg landscape, subsidized by the provincial and national authorities.

A project as the one at Neercanne might greatly benefit from a thorough study of our own concepts and views on gardens, landscape and nature, and of the way we want to assess their historical and present-day importance.

The garden is indeed a monument in its own right, but its importance exceeds the limits of ownership – and the landscape was, and is, largely dependent on the castle which dominates the whole with its terraces. Reconciliation of what are considered to be opposites may very well be the real challenge of the Neercanne project, on which many of the more detailed decisions will depend. If we proceed with good taste and understanding, we may bring about the revival not only of a unique garden, but also of a remarkable landscape where nature and culture may be enhanced by blending them into a meaningful whole, rich in contrasts.

---

1 Compare the text of a symposium on this subject held in 1995: *De eeuw van Thijsse. 100 jaar natuurbeleving en natuurbescherming.*
2 See, among others, Bekkers, 'Het Hollandse landschap in de tuinkunst'.
3 See e.g. Feddes, *Oorden van onthouding*, *De architectuur van de ruimte* and De Jong, 'Gewilde natuur'.
4 See *Het Cultuurlandschap*.
5 For the most detailed research on Neercanne, see Brummel, '«Natuur met kunst vereent»'.
6 See the collections of drawings of Neercanne in the Historical Topographical Atlas of the Municipal Archives, Maastricht, among others the works by Van Gulpen, Schaepkens, Lefebre and Semays. For the daguerreotype, see Coppens and Albers, *Een camera vol stilte.*
7 For the evaluation of engraved and painted pictures of Dutch gardens in the seventeenth century, see De Jong and Dominicus-van Soest, *Aardse Paradijzen.*
8 For details, see Brummel, '«Natuur met kunst vereent»'.
9 For the various developments in the Limburg landscape and the position there of gardens, horticulture, agriculture, viniculture, etc., see Renes, *De geschiedenis van het Zuidlimburgse cultuurlandschap*; for gardening and social status, see De Jong, *Natuur en kunst*. During the symposium, Carla Oldenburger drew attention to the terraced gardens of the Slavante cloister near Maastricht. She concluded that Neercanne should be interpreted from a regional point of view only instead of taking a general Dutch, or even an international, perspective as a point of reference. See Oldenburger-Ebbers, 'Overwegingen'. To Dutch experiments with forestry, viniculture, etc., I hope to return in a new book on the Dutch tradition of gardening, to be published with Yale University Press.
10 On Johan Maurits van Nassau-Siegen, see the material collected in *Soweit der Erdkreis reicht*, and on his gardens, the material presented by Diedenhofen in that catalogue and in Diedenhofen, 'Johan Maurits and His Gardens'; on Potsdam and surroundings, see *Potsdamer Schlösser und Gärten*, Kap. 1, pp. 13-100.
11 De Jong, '«Een teyken van den soeten vreed». Zur Interpretation des «Eisernen Mannes» am Springenberg', in *Soweit der Erdkreis reicht*, pp. 165-88.
12 For these devices, see De Jong, *Natuur en kunst*, pp. 49-52; on the importance of seeing and looking in the gardens of Cleves, see Diedenhofen, '«Belvedere»'.
13 See *Bijdragen en mededeelingen.*
14 For Italian and French models, see Steenbergen and Reh, *Architecture and Landscape*, Ch. 1 ('The Poetics of the Rational. The Italian Renaissance Villa') and 11 ('The Magics of the Formal. The 17th-Century French Residence'). For the influence of Pliny, see De La Ruffinière du Prey, *The Villas of Pliny.*
15 For William III and Bentinck's letters, see De Jong, *Natuur en kunst*, Ch. 3.
16 See De Zeeuw, Steenbergen and De Jong, 'De Beemster'.
17 For the 'grammar' of formal gardens and their relationship with the landscape, see Steenbergen and Reh, op.cit., Ch. 1 and 11; for ideas on geometry, see also De Jong, *Natuur en Kunst*, Ch. 2.
18 For the archaeological evidence, see the documentation at the Technical University Delft, Department of Restoration, partly presented in Snelder, *Château Neercanne.*
19 I owe this quotation from Evelyn's letter to Robert Berkeley (of 16 June 1686) to Professor Douglas

Chambers, Trinity College, Toronto, who is preparing an annotated edition of the Evelyn letters. See his contribution to the forthcoming volume on Evelyn, Dumbarton Oaks, Washington, D.C.; for an interpretation, see De Jong, 'Vackra igenom konst'.

20 Brummel, '«Natuur met kunst vereent»', p. 99. The parterre at Clingendaal was inspired by the main parterre in the garden of Saint-Germain-en-Laye, after a design by Boyceau and modernized in 1665 by Le Nôtre; see V. Bezemer-Sellers in *The Anglo Dutch Garden*, cat. no. 53.

21 For this 'restoration', see Van den Bossche, *De tuinen van Alden Biesen*.

22 See Renes, *De geschiedenis van het Zuidlimburgse cultuurlandschap*.

23 See M. Dominicus-van Soest in *The Anglo Dutch Garden*, cat. nos. 44-52. For the document by Johan Maurits van Nassau-Siegen, see ibid., p. 335.

De architectuur van de ruimte. Nota over het architectuurbeleid 1997-2000. Compiled by Platform Architectuurbeleid, with contributions by Fred Feddes. September 1996.

The Anglo Dutch Garden in the Age of William and Mary / De Gouden Eeuw van de Hollandse tuinkunst. Special double issue of *Journal of Garden History*, 8 (1988), 2 and 3, pp. 1-341. J. D. Hunt and E. de Jong, eds.

Bekkers, G. 'Het Hollandse landschap in de tuinkunst. Plantengemeenschappen als medium bij het ontwerp, 1900-45'. In Erik de Jong (ed.). *Tuinkunst. Nederlands jaarboek voor de geschiedenis van de tuin- en landschapsarchitectuur*, 1 (1995), pp. 95-121.

Bossche, Herman van den. *De tuinen van Alden Biesen. Een nieuwe hof naar oud model. Monumenten en landschappen*, 10 (1991), 3, n.p.

Bijdragen en mededeelingen van het Historisch Genootschap. Utrecht, 1887. Vol. 10, pp. 227-336.

Brummel, Klazien. '«Natuur met kunst vereent»; historisch onderzoek naar de vroeg 18e-eeuwse situatie van de terrastuin van Kasteel Neercanne'. In *Bulletin KNOB*, 92 (1993), 4, pp. 89-114.

Coppens, Jan, and A. Albers. *Een camera vol stilte. Nederland in het begin van de fotografie 1839-1875.* Amsterdam: Meulenhoff, 1976.

De eeuw van Thijsse. 100 jaar natuurbeleving en natuurbescherming. Amsterdam: Heimans en Thijsse Stichting, 1996.

Diedenhofen, W. 'Johan Maurits and His Gardens'. In E. van den Boogaart (ed.). *Johan Maurits van Nassau-Siegen 1604-1679. A Humanist Prince in Europe and Brazil.* The Hague, 1979, pp. 197-236.

Diedenhofen, W. '«Belvedere», or the Principle of Seeing and Looking in the Gardens of Johan Maurits van Nassau-Siegen at Cleves'. In *The Dutch Garden in the Seventeenth Century.* Washington DC: Dumbarton Oaks Research Library and Collection, 1990, pp. 49-81.

Feddes, Fred. *Oorden van onthouding.* Rotterdam: NAi, 1996.

Het cultuurlandschap. Een terreinverkenning over landschapsarchitectuur en cultuurbeleid. Compiled by Dirk Sijmons and Eric Luijten. Utrecht: H + N + S, 1994.

Jong, Erik de. *Natuur en kunst. Nederlandse tuin- en landschapsarchitectuur 1650-1740.* 2nd imp. Bussum, 1995.

Jong, Erik de, and Marleen Dominicus-van Soest. *Aardse paradijzen* 1. *De tuin in de Nederlandse kunst 15de tot 18de eeuw.* Gent, 1996.

Jong, Erik de. 'Gewilde natuur. Over de betekenis van ecologie en landschapsarchitectuur. Nature in Demand. On the Importance of Ecology and Landscape Architecture'. In *Archis*, 1996, no. 10, pp. 60-66.

Jong, Erik de. 'Vackra igenom konst och arbete gjorda platser. Understanding Dutch Gardens and Landscapes from the Seventeenth and Early Eighteenth Century'. In *Lustgården. Yearbook of the Swedish Society for Dendrology and Park Culture*, 76 (1996), pp. 5-30.

Oldenburger-Ebbers, C. 'Overwegingen bij het herstel van de tuinen van Neercanne'. In *Cascade. Bulletin voor tuinhistorie*, 5 (1996), pp. 43-49.

Potsdamer Schlösser und Gärten. Bau- und Gartenkunst vom 17. bis 20. Jahrhundert. Generaldirektion der Stiftung Schlösser und Gärten Potsdam-Sanssouci, 1993.

Renes, J. *De geschiedenis van het Zuidlimburgse cultuurlandschap.* 2 vols. Assen / Maastricht: Van Gorcum, 1988.

Ruffinière du Prey, Pierre de La. *The Villas of Pliny. From Antiquity to Posterity.* Chicago: University of Chicago Press, 1994.

Snelder, W. J. A. *Château Neercanne. Voorlopig onderzoeksverslag 1989 / Werkgroep Restauratie.* Eys, 1991.

Soweit der Erdkreis Reicht. Johann Moritz von Nassau-Siegen 1604-1679. Catalogue edited by Guido de Werd. Cleves, 1979.

Steenbergen, Clemens, and Wouter Reh. *Architecture and Landscape. The Design Experiment of the Great European Gardens and Landscapes.* Bussum: Thoth, 1996.

Zeeuw, Peter de, Clemens Steenbergen, and Erik de Jong. 'De Beemster. Een arena van natuur, kunst en techniek'. In Toon Lauwen and Tjeerd Boersma (eds.). *Nederland als kunstwerk. Vijf eeuwen bouwen door ingenieurs.* Rotterdam: NAi, 1995, pp. 153-68.

Neercanne: Towards a definition of a dynamic composition and its characteristics

FRITS VAN VOORDEN
& BASTIAAN KWAST

THE VALLEY OF the small river Jeker forms an impressive decor for the castle and the terraced gardens of Neercanne. Anyone who would attempt to improve this work of art without overplaying his hand is very courageous. A re-creation of Van Dopff's garden in minute detail includes by definition a certain amount of speculation.

1 *The shadowy world between original design and current state*

Where the original design remains vague despite archival research and surgically precise local digging, we must rely on imagination and specialized knowledge. At the same time, the blind spots in our knowledge make restoration a design project, aiming to bridge the gap between the shadowy world of the paper garden (the archival and topographical sources) and the current situation. Both have qualities which can be reinforced as part of a restoration by a precise 'reading' of the current state of the terraces and surrounding landscape in the context of information gathered from archives, archaeological research and soil surveys. To arrive at a just proposal for the second and third terraces, the objective of the current owner, it is useful to consider the gardens and the countryside in their relationship to one another. The evolution of time also deserves consideration: why should all of the changes that have taken place since the woods and gardens were planted be rejected as unauthentic?

Nature in the Netherlands is a rare and rightly cherished entity. A problem resulting from this is the image that we expect from nature: any man-made intervention must remain invisible. This apparent contradiction between nature and culture has long been a roadblock to an open discussion of the conservation/restoration of the Neercanne landscape. From the very first moment that the provisional restoration plan for the castle gardens was announced – at the end of the 1980s – nature conservation and monument protection societies have taken up their positions. Proponents of restoration from the angle of art history were suspected of lacking respect for the value of nature. On the other hand, those impassioned by an unspoiled, picturesque natural idyll rejected any form of cultural interference. The conflicting interests of nature and culture preservation, which are particularly sharp where the fourth terrace is concerned, came increasingly to the foreground during this process of debate. As a result, the possibility of achieving an integrated restoration of natural and cultural elements was lost out of sight, and both the gardens and the meadows have been neglected (soil contamination, river-bank and stream pollution). The stone rim of the mirror pond in the fourth terrace, for example, is being destroyed by the surrounding tree roots (among them willows which are recent pioneer vegetation). Even a modest attempt to maintain the traces of the early-eighteenth-century grounds would now require a large-scale effort.

What follows is a brief analysis in words and pictures of the spatial relationship between castle, outbuildings, gardens, woods, pastures and the Jeker. The structural components of the evolved eighteenth-century landscape are waiting to be re-covered under a thin layer of earth, while some elements are still visible. Thus they form, in our opinion, more reliable 'material' for renewal than speculative reconstruction of long-disappeared ornamentation: better no baroque than false baroque.

2 *Movement and differences in level*

The refined placement of the gardens against the hillside may be considered in the way the differences in levels have been articulated to give movement through the property a theatrical dimension. The terraced gardens remain largely hidden to the chance passer-by behind the impressive formation of the fortified retaining wall. But once the passer-by has gone beyond the path between the third and the second terrace, he is taken briefly into the heart of the composition. At this point the road joins the rectangular lines of the plan and forms its only visible extension until a point beyond the bounds of the gardens: an anchoring of the design in the far-away countryside, running parallel to the linear direction of the valley. Stylized fortifications were a regular feature of gardens at the time (compare Vanbrugh's design for the gardens of Blenheim, a present from Queen Anne to the hero who defeated the French in 1704, the Duke of Marlborough). The access lanes, in contrast, do not fit in with the rectangularly designed grid. To bridge the differences in level between the road and the house in a relaxed fashion, the lanes are almost parallel to the contour lines. Where necessary to heighten the drama or increase comfort, the designer took the liberty of departing from the seeming autonomy of the plan to following the dictates of the topography. The northern access lane, for example, splits off from the road between Maastricht and Canne, climbs slightly and ends between a rock wall and the entrance side of the castle. Only after entering the hall does one see the gardens, the river and the hills far behind. This theatrical direction of the entrance gives the 'back side' of the house, which is turned towards the rock wall, the status of a front. The playful use of levels is repeated in miniature with the third terrace. The – original! – slope of the ground level in conjunction with the – also original – height of the eastern wall offers a changing perspective. If one stands in the long western half of the garden, there is an unimpeded view of the Jeker valley; if one finds oneself in the eastern half, however, only the view of the village of Canne (the church tower) and the castle remains, due to the high wall.

This demonstrates that very careful use was made of what the site had to offer: literally, the relief and existing constructions, and figuratively, the military activities of which Van Dopff was the hub, for example.

At the same time, there is the influence of cultural notions based on precedents from architectural history. It is impossible to determine the extent to which this influenced the original conception without more knowledge about the design and the person who commissioned the construction.

3 Green pastures

Since the historical situation is unclear, it seems legitimate to give the existing qualities their due, whether they be authentic or not. One example of this is the current blending of the terraces and the surrounding cultural landscape, as it is seen from the castle, into one whole. Covering the third and fourth terraces with a carpeting of grass will add greatly to the above-mentioned effect. In that way they will acquire the character of small-scale, walled-in fields. The effect created by a carefully considered, organized outside area in with the still visible remnants of the geometric pattern (property boundaries, walls and lines of trees, the large pond) refers to the order in the total landscape rather than a forgotten historical image. This strong relationship between foreground and background will be at issue once the terraces will be restored. Although the contrast between the man-made terraces and the cultural landscape outside them was once maximized, the larger visual and conceptual entity of the terraces and fields which has evolved over the years is too remarkable in its own right to be destroyed by a modern intervention.

It would seem as if time has created a new concept in Neercanne's landscape architecture. The villa is now placed directly in the landscape of agrarian production. There are beautiful examples of this in the Veneto area: the Palladian villas. The reduction of the formal garden to a plinth around the house and a single long lane which led through the surrounding countryside sanctions, as it were, the aesthetic qualities of the agricultural setting in and of itself. Anyone who has seen Neercanne – from close by or inside the house – will recognize this ode to the agricultural setting and will need to weigh the value of what history has created against the value of the original early-eighteenth-century design.

4 The role of the star-shaped wood in the composition of the garden

A distinctive characteristic of the gardens is the star-shaped copse which was heralded by Le Bruyn in his perspective of 1715. If it was carried out in more or less this form, which is not certain, there would have been parallel to the main axis an almost equal axis which connected an obelisk, an amphitheatre cut into the marl and the northern border of the fourth terrace. Le Bruyn recognized this interplay of shifting accents by choosing the standpoint of his perspective exactly in the extension of this line. If it was visible from the valley, this placement of garden ornaments to the side of the main axis must have made a great contribution to the dynamics of the composition. It is not just a matter of a parallel displacement. It is possible that there was a diagonal lane that led from the house to the pavilion on the western plateau edge, probably one of the few with a decline acceptable to walkers.

The pattern of the lanes has been lost, however, in the struggle between geometry and nature. According to reports, remnants of structures have been found. The provisional exclusion of the star-shaped copse in a reconstruction plan, as a result of divided ownership, forces us to interpret the presumed original design. Because what, in the view of a designer, is the value of the perfect restitution of a partial composition? A polished reconstruction of the four terraces might lead to an unauthentic emphasis on the symmetrical layout of the gardens on the two sides of the main axis. Recognition of the structure of the eighteenth-century design justifies a greater freedom in rearrangement of the terraces with complete conservation of the historical layer, if necessary with the addition of a protective layer of earth.

The current property distribution and the lack of clarity about the original state of the gardens and the landscape make complete reconstruction impossible. Wherever structural components such as dikes, paths and the two ponds (either above ground or not) are found, ornamentation has not stood the injuries of time. The key to restoration lies in unearthing the framework of the composition without covering this with a layer of speculative details. A rough proposal for the restoration of each terrace was made during the workshops.

We offer here a spatial analysis of the structure of the Neercanne garden in word and image combined.

The spatial and architectural themes of the composition are given in a series of plans and analytic drawings which are presented as an independent whole on pp. 55-59. The documentation has been put together in the CAD laboratory of the Department of Architecture of the Technical University Delft and supplemented with drawings and sketches by the authors.

SPATIAL ANALYSIS OF THE STRUCTURE OF THE NEERCANNE GARDEN

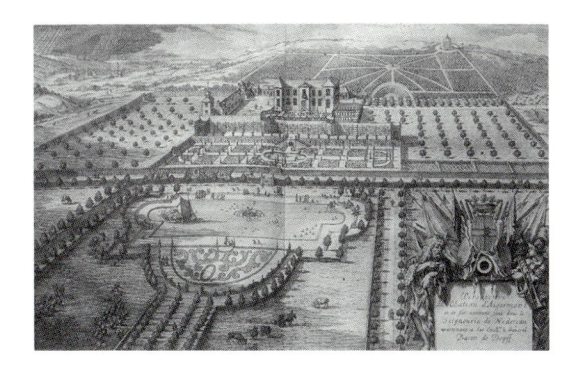

1*a* G. Le Bruyn. *Perspective of Neercanne*. Engraving. In F. Halma, *Het Kasteel van Aigermont etc.*, Leeuwarden, 1715. (Photo: University Library, Amsterdam)

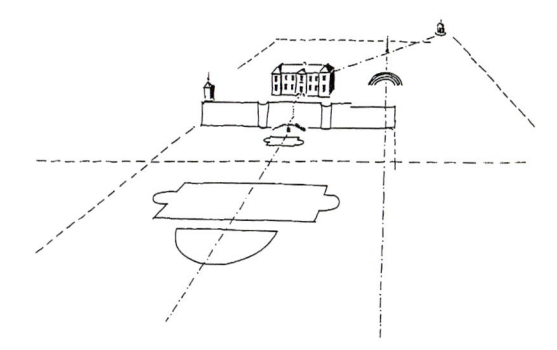

1*b* The main axis and the second axis between the star-shaped copse and the fourth terrace. The architectural elements of the upper garden are the pavilion, the obelisk and the amphitheatre built into the marl. (Original sketch by B. Kwast)

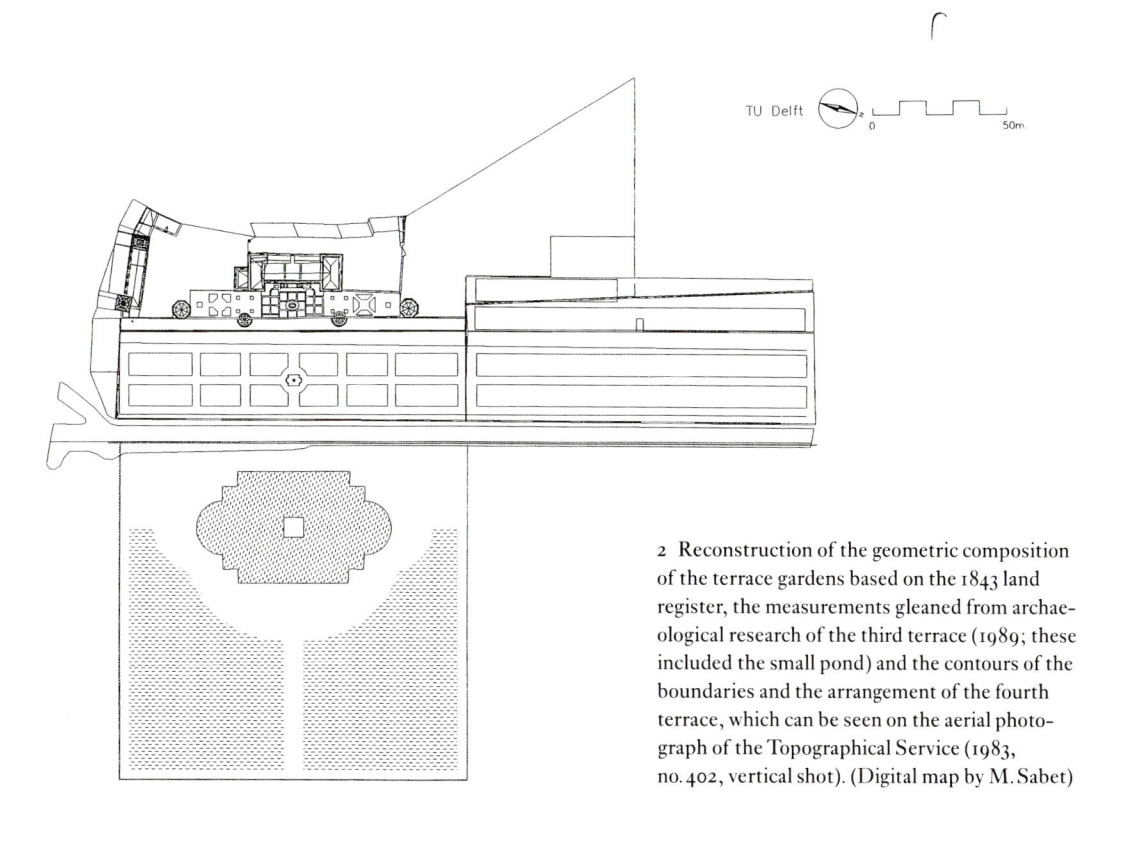

2 Reconstruction of the geometric composition of the terrace gardens based on the 1843 land register, the measurements gleaned from archaeological research of the third terrace (1989; these included the small pond) and the contours of the boundaries and the arrangement of the fourth terrace, which can be seen on the aerial photograph of the Topographical Service (1983, no. 402, vertical shot). (Digital map by M. Sabet)

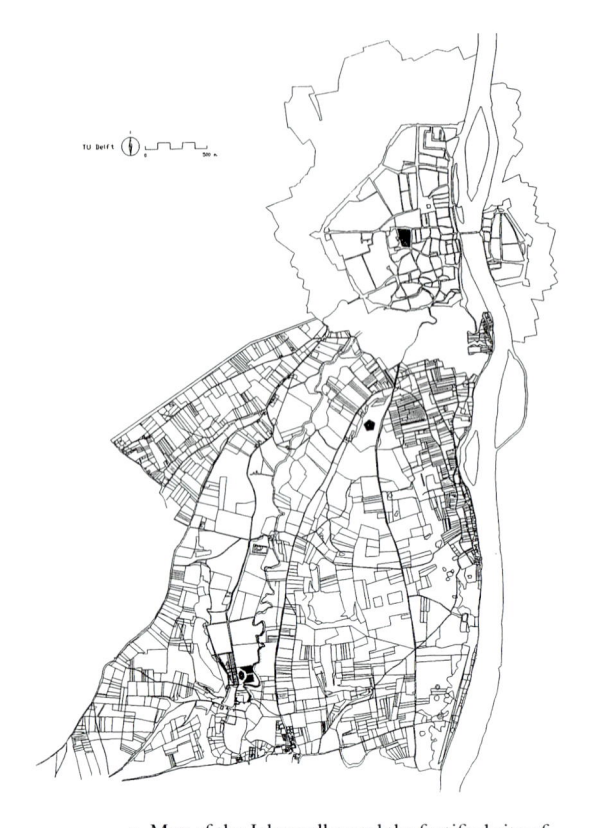

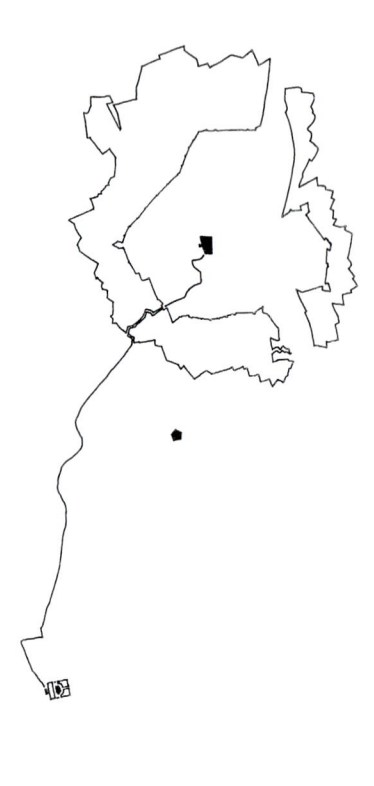

3 Map of the Jeker valley and the fortified city of Maastricht, ca.1840 (source: Land Register; Archives of Maastricht, Hasselt and Roermond/ Apeldoorn). Noteworthy architectural and spatial elements indicated are, from north to south, the Vrijthof and the military Hoofdwacht (main guardhouse), the St. Peter fort and Neercanne castle. (Digital map by M. Sabet)

4a In her article on Neercanne – '«Natuur met kunst vereent»', in *Bulletin KNOB*, 92 (1993), 4, p.106 – Klazien Brummel indicated the theatrical qualities of the road from the city to Neercanne. Van Dopff was also the builder of the St. Peter fort (constructed 1701-2; for technical details, see L.J. Morreau, *Bolwerk der Nederlanden*, Assen, 1979, p.241). The road from the Vrijthof (Place d'Armes) to Neercanne is roughly reproduced (direction north-south).

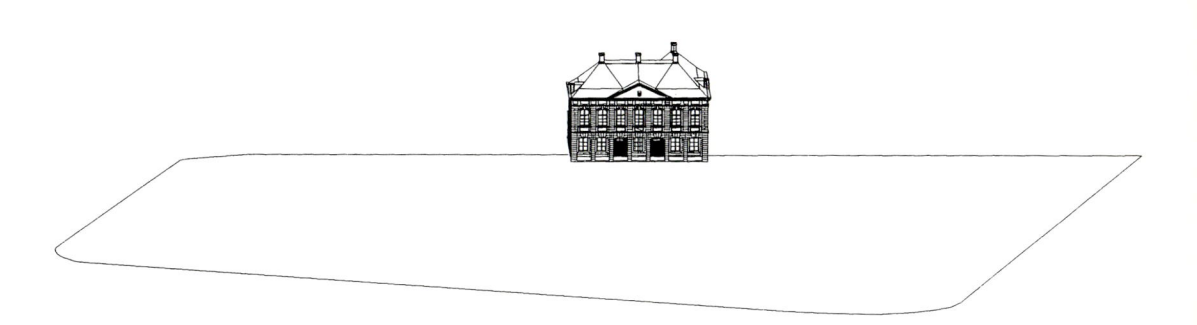

4*b* Architectural diagram of the Hoofdwacht with the contours of the exercise grounds of the Vrijthof. The 'Hoofdwacht' which is represented here was built in 1736 on about the same spot of an older building which had the same function as 'vieux Corps de garde'. The composition of the main guard building and exercise grounds at the foot of the massive St. Servatius church was already functioning during the governorship of Van Dopff. From the still extant specifications of 26 September 1736, it is apparent that the foundations were built of 'bloques sablonneuses de la montagne de St. Pierre de Nederkan ou de Montenaque'. The building itself is in Namur stone (*Monumenten van geschiedenis en Kunst [Geïllustreerde Beschrijving]*, *Municipality of Maastricht*, first instalment, The Hague, 1926). (Digital drawing by T. van Amsterdam)

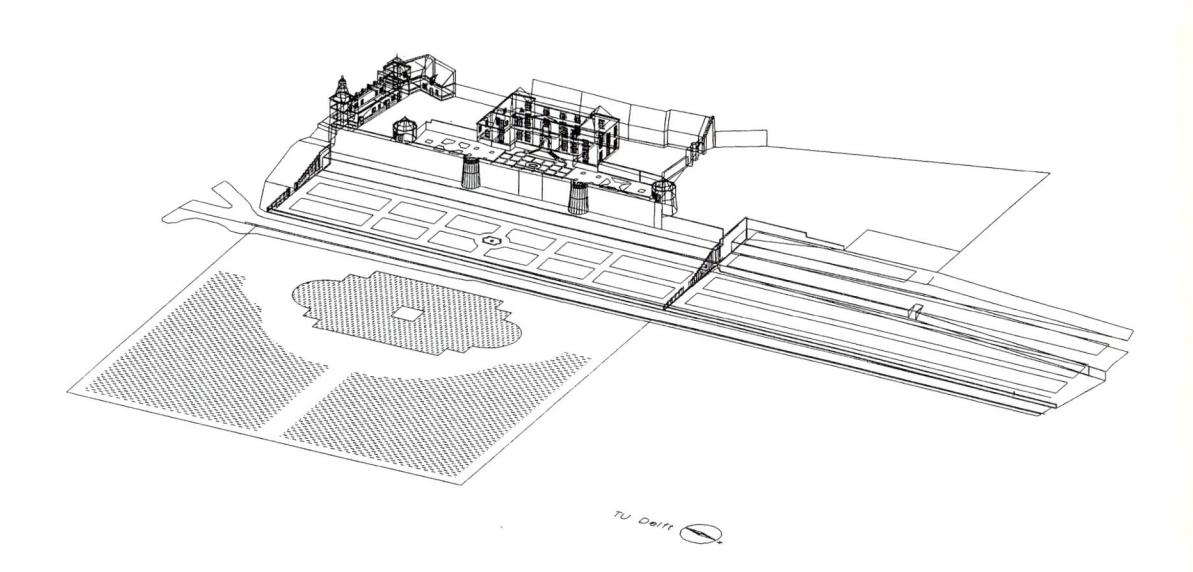

4*c* Architectural diagram of Neercanne castle and terrace gardens with an indication of the original composition. Bird's-eye view of illustration 2 (for the source see under fig. 2).

5 Digitalized map of Neercanne castle and the village of Canne, ca. 1843, based on the 1843 land register (Hasselt cadastre). (Digital map by M. Sabet)

6 Sketch of the castle with the retaining wall with military details between the first and second terraces. In the foreground, the third terrace, situated in the natural surface level of the Jeker valley. (Drawing by F. van Voorden, based on a photograph at the Rijksdienst voor de Monumentenzorg, Zeist)

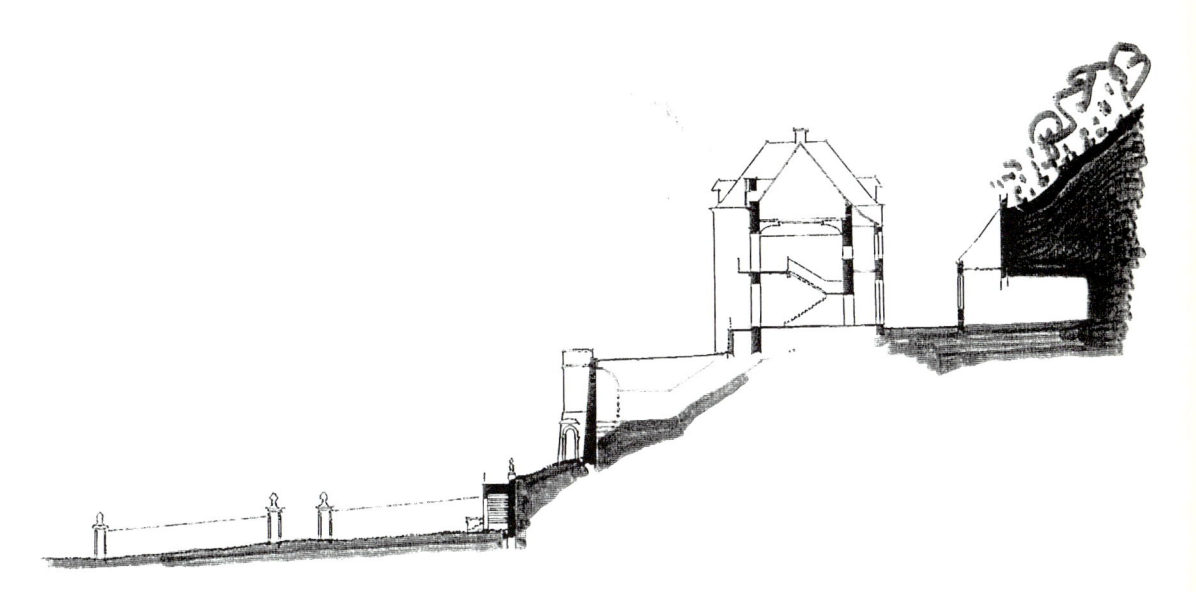

7 Cross section of (from right to left) the Cannerberg with annexes built into and against the mountain, plus the entrance to the grottoes, the castle, the first terrace, the fortified retaining wall, the second terrace and the walled third terrace. (Drawing by F. van Voorden; source: *Geïllustreerde Beschrijving, Municipality of Maastricht*, The Hague, 1953, illustration XXXI, after measurements of H. van Beveren of 1946)

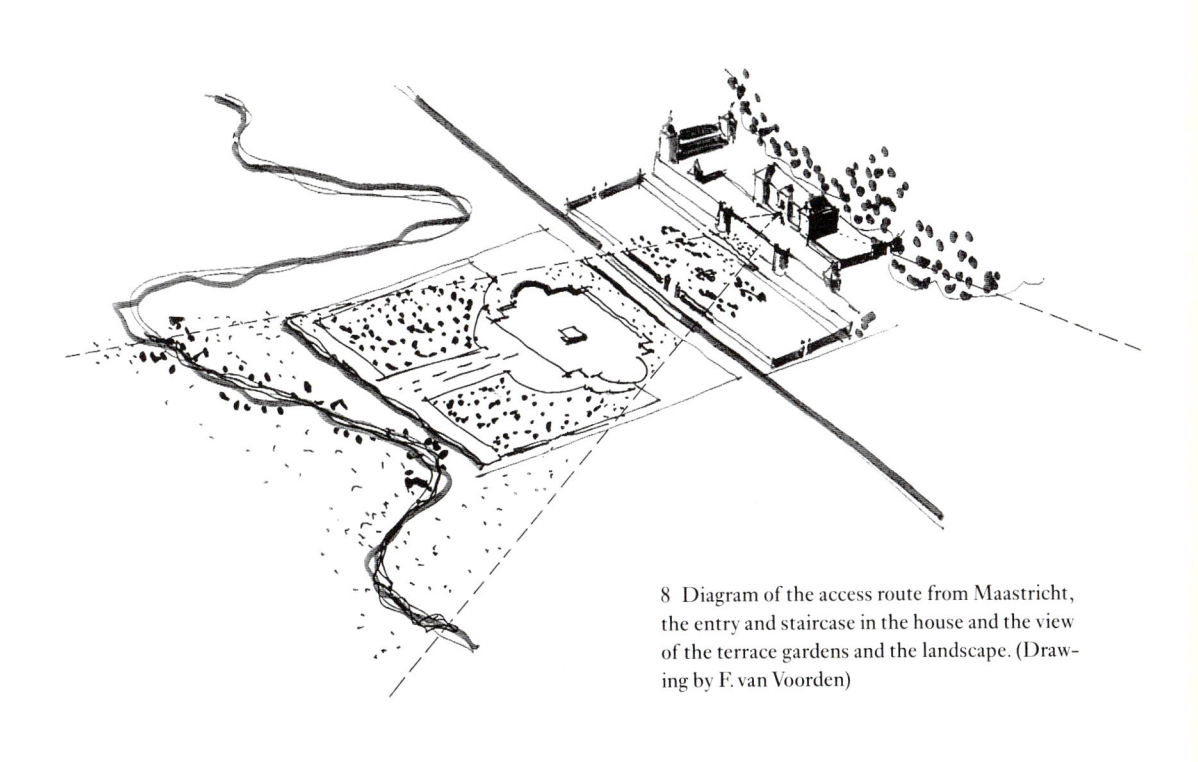

8 Diagram of the access route from Maastricht, the entry and staircase in the house and the view of the terrace gardens and the landscape. (Drawing by F. van Voorden)

1

'Original fabric' or 'original design intent'? The unresolved dilemma in planting conservation

MARK LAIRD

THE CONSERVATION OF historic gardens, like all forms of conservation, should be primarily concerned with the protection, recording and repair of 'original fabric'.[1] By 'fabric' we mean the physical remains of the past that have come down to us today. Whether in the form of built or planted features, these venerable remains are, after all, our only tangible link to a past that cannot be remade. It is for this reason that extraordinary care should be taken when 'garden restoration' is on the agenda; for sooner or later, restoration will involve some destruction of original fabric, sometimes through archaeology but often through reconstruction.[2]

Caution is required for other reasons too. There is the danger of losing the special quality of repose that can only come from the passage of time, the ageing of stone or the maturing of trees. Moreover, the overlays or accretions – even the 'accidents' of growth – often produce a visual and textual richness that cannot be replicated. Above all, there is always a risk of 'inventing' the past when, even after exhaustive research and site investigation, this or that detail remains unknown or conjectural. The problem of conjecture is especially acute with regard to the planting of the seventeenth or eighteenth century; for the *plate-bande*, flower bed or shrubbery will tend to leave next to no trace of its former horticultural character.[3]

However, if we were to accept that all garden conservation should be reduced to protecting what survives from the past – in other words, a philosophy of 'minimal intervention' – we would be left with a very impoverished version of Renaissance, Baroque or Picturesque garden design. The later overlays would predominate and our view of the past would remain distorted by their imprint. The complete disappearance of historic forms of planting in their original condition – the parterres, bosquets and shrubberies – is especially troubling in this respect. Unlike the architecture or fine art of the seventeenth and eighteenth centuries, the planting in historic sites of that same period has largely

1 The parterre at Hanbury Hall – an evocation of the past in 1995. (Photo: Mark Laird)

vanished. And so we are confronted with a huge dilemma: how do we regain 'original design intent' without destroying 'original fabric'?[4]

The recovery of lost forms of planting has been one important impetus behind the wave of garden restoration projects in the 1980s and 1990s (figs. 2 and 3).[5] While some of these projects have been more successful than others, the important point is that every restoration scheme has involved losses as well as gains. The purpose of this contribution and the conference as a whole should be to find a way of assessing those risks and opportunities before the irrevocable processes of 'restoration' are already under way.

In the first part of this essay, I shall offer an overview of various restoration projects that have taken place over the past twenty years in Western Europe: from the early efforts at Schwetzingen, Westbury Court and Het Loo to the more recent work at Tredegar House, Hanbury Hall and Kirby Hall. I shall review the progress in methodology through the medium of planting. For planting restoration highlights some crucial dilemmas in conservation – the problem of conjecture, the dimension of growth, the loss of original plant material. This topic will offer an opportunity to explore the tensions between the ideals of pure conservation on the one hand and the attractions of radical reconstruction on the other hand. The second part of my talk will cover the philosophical

2

and practical implications of some of those dilemmas; while the third part provides a constructive look at the various options that present themselves to the responsible curator of the 1990s. These thoughts may be of some help in reviewing the specific case of the Neercanne Castle project.

1 *Reviving gardens in the 1950s to the 1970s*

From the 1950s to the 1970s there were a few isolated attempts at reviving the original appearance of some seventeenth-century gardens. It is easy to dismiss them now as 'period gardens', based more on fancy than on fact. However, all conservation is constrained by the thinking of the time and the technology of the day. Indeed, I believe these early projects should be viewed as vitally important steps in the direction of today's approach. At Pitmedden, Aberdeenshire, for example, the National Trust for Scotland began work in 1956 to remake the Great Garden of Sir Alexander Seeton, first formed in 1664-75.[6] They based the design of the parterres on a view of Holyroodhouse in 1647. These parterres were planted up with masses of bedding plants such as French marigolds (*Tagetes patula*). In other words, there was much latitude in borrowing another layout from another date, and much licence in using twentieth-

2 View from the reconstructed Turkish Tent at Painshill Park, with restored Grotto in the middleground and restored Gothic Temple in the background in 1995. (Photo: Mark Laird)

3 Reconstructed shrubbery below the Gothic Temple at Painshill Park in 1995. (Photo: Mark Laird)

century styles of planting. The French marigold may have been available by the seventeenth century, but it would never have been used in such blankets (fig. 4).[7]

In 1978 the National Trust followed a somewhat similar approach in replanting the parterre and wilderness at Ham House in Surrey (fig. 5).[8] Here the planting features were clearly derived from evidence of the site as laid out for the Duke of Lauderdale in the 1670s. However, the interpretation of horticultural effect was still influenced by modern taste or by the constraints of modern maintenance. Hence the use of massed planting in muted hues – far from the late-seventeenth-century ideal of mixed colours – was simply a variation on the bright parterres of Pitmedden. The use of garden archaeology never occurred as an issue in either site. Over the past few years it has become apparent – from a follow-up study of the replanting at Ham – that potential evidence in the ground (or, for that matter, above ground) may have been destroyed through the initial clearance of the 1970s.[9]

In contrast, the reconstruction of the Leonsberg garden outside Stuttgart did take advantage of archaeology as early as the 1970s (fig. 6).[10] However, the project was not overly concerned with using original flowers in 'authentic' ways. Indeed, attention to 'authenticity' of horticultural effect was first apparent in

4

the National Trust's rescue of the derelict layout of Westbury Court in Gloucestershire.[11] By juggling the position of the parterre in Maynard Colchester's original garden of 1695-1705 (altered c.1715), the Trust had, of course, reconstructed a notional rather than actual layout of the past. However, the attention to horticultural accuracy that followed the initial intervention of 1973 was a considerable advance in method. The use of old varieties (the double wallflower, *Cheiranthus cheiri flore pleno*, for example), original types of espalier fruit-tree and original tulip species (as well as 'look-alike' tulip cultivars of the nineteenth century) helped to make Westbury a delightful place for all flower-lovers (figs. 7 and 8). Whether these 'original' plants were disposed according to a pattern or system that was 'authentic' to the period, however, still remained largely beyond consideration.

INCREASING INTEREST IN 'ORIGINAL' PLANTS   By the early 1980s the interest in these planting systems was coming to the forefront. In the reconstruction of the parterres at Schwetzingen, near Heidelberg, much use was made of A.-J. Dezallier d'Argenville's instructions for planting up a *plate-bande* or flower border.[12] These instructions, first published in the 1722 edition of *La*

4 The Great Garden at Pitmedden, Aberdeenshire, re-created by The National Trust for Scotland from 1956 onwards in 1979. (Photo: Mark Laird)

5 Detail of replanted parterre at Ham House, Surrey in 1980. (Photo: Mark Laird)

Théorie et la pratique du jardinage, were still endorsed in the 1760 edition, and this corresponded well to the making of the parterres shown in Johann Ludwig Petri's 1753 plan for Kurfürst Carl Theodor. Here, for the first time, was an approximation to the effect of mixed colours: what Dezallier d'Argenville called 'le mélange émaillé de toutes sortes de couleurs' (fig. 9).[13] However, the French method of creating three decorations per season[14] – spring, summer and autumn – was condensed into two, with pansies used over winter, and the concern for original plant types (as demonstrated at Westbury Court) was ignored in favour of easy upkeep. Modern cultivars, and even a few species introduced after the eighteenth century, were a major part of the planting palette. This may have compromised the 'authenticity' of the display, but not the dramatic visual quality of the whole parterre.

Modelling a *plate-bande* after a specific planting system was also in evidence in the replanting of the flower borders in the parterres at Brühl – the garden originally designed in 1728 by Dominique Girard for Kurfürst Clemens August.[15] This replanting took place in 1984. The model was the 1693 plan for the Grand Trianon, preserved in the Bibliothèque Nationale in Paris. The planting plan demonstrated a method of disposing bulbs and summer perennials on a grid so as to produce colourful rhythms. However, in place of the ori-

6

ginal lilies, Greek valerian and sweet williams, etc., the gardeners at Brühl produced 86,000 summer bedding plants like calceolaria, salvia and ageratum. Once again the splendid visual impact was created with an eye to easy maintenance (fig. 10).

By contrast, the replanting of the flower borders in the reconstructed parterres at Het Loo displayed a concern for original planting method and original planting palette.[16] The disposition of bulbs, flowers and evergreens, as well as climbers on stakes, was based not so much on an original planting plan from the time of Daniel Marot, but more on the engravings of the period – for example, Laurens Scherm's view of the parterres c.1700. Those engravings suggested the dominance of a sparse style of planting. Each plant was displayed as an individual specimen, not primarily as units of colour massed together. Great care was taken in using original plants – the double forms of columbine (*Aquilegia vulgaris plena*), for example, or the purple moth-mullein (*Verbascum phoeniceum*). Where conjecture occurred, choices were directed by analogies from other sites or from other contemporary art forms – the colour schemes of the interior décor, for example. Thus, a methodology for replanting was developed that stands up to scrutiny today (fig. 11). However, for some, the destruction of original fabric – the loss of built and planted features from the nineteenth- and

7

6 The replanted parterre of the Pomeranzengarten, Leonberg near Stuttgart in 1981. (Photo: Mark Laird)

7 The replanted walled garden at Westbury Court in 1991. (Photo: Mark Laird)

twentieth-century landscaping, and the loss of evidence in the ground – remains a concern that was not addressed in the reconstruction philosophy of the late 1970s and early 1980s.

Jan Woudstra has illustrated how the team at Hampton Court attempted to marry advances in archaeology with the methodology of planting research first established at Het Loo.[17] The success of the archaeological approach was overwhelming, and today we are able to enjoy the Wren façade with its appropriate planting (figs. 12 and 13).[18] Thus, in most respects, the reconstruction of the Privy Garden serves as a model for the 1990s. However, the unusual level of evidence, both archival and archaeological, makes Hampton Court highly unusual. Most sites will fall well short of providing detailed lists of plants, or detailed engravings of flower borders. And each site is affected by its own particular circumstances that only allow room for certain types of intervention.

RECENT ENGLISH PROJECTS   Three recent projects in England underscore those variables. At Hanbury Hall near Droitwich in Worcestershire, work commenced in the autumn of 1993 to reinstate the early-eighteenth-century garden. The eventual replanting – very much attuned to new realities – can be regarded as something of an evocation of the original rather than a reconstruction in the sense of Hampton Court (fig.1). Meanwhile, at Tredegar House near Newport in Wales, an archaeological investigation revealed two layers dating back to the turn of the eighteenth century (with the original forecourt entirely intact).[19] However, as the owners of the property, Newport Borough Council, were unable to proceed with a comprehensive excavation, a provisional reconstruction of one layout for the Orangery Garden was instituted in 1992 (fig.14). By placing this parterre on top of a protective layer of 'Terram', the landscape team attempted to allow for later, more exhaustive analysis. The fact that several layers of parterre, dating back over several centuries, were found preserved one on top of the other at Castle Bromwich Hall near Birmingham lends credibility to the idea of protecting archaeological data by imposing a new level on the site.[20]

Such protection is clearly desirable. At Kirby Hall in Northamptonshire, the archaeological data were largely destroyed in the excavations of 1935 – excavations that were meant to help reconstruct the parterres of the 1690s. When Brian Dix recently investigated what survived beneath the reconstruction, he found insufficient remains to undertake another 'Privy Garden' – despite the excellent plant lists of 1685-1706.[21] Whether English Heritage's subsequent decision to replace the rather dull reconstruction of the 1930s with a recon-

8 *Cheiranthus cheiri flore pleno* in the walled garden at Westbury Court in 1991. (Photo: Mark Laird)
9 The reconstructed parterre at Schwetzingen, near Heidelberg in 1983. (Photo: Mark Laird)
10 The *plate-bande* of the parterre at Brühl in 1991. (Photo: Mark Laird)

structed layout based on London and Wise's contemporary grass parterres at Longleat seems a good solution, is surely open to debate (fig. 15). This literal transposition involves issues of congruity between garden and architecture, issues of scale, and issues of 'invention' or 'fabrication'. By comparison, the work in the Privy Garden at Hampton Court appears solidly grounded in the particularities of the site.

Yet the reconstruction of the parterre at Hampton Court raises other issues beyond verification of evidence. There are, for example, the twin issues discussed in my introduction: the loss of 'original fabric' and the loss of 'repose' – that numinous sense of place, that feeling of age, that timelessness that comes from the passage of time. In historical reality, the Privy Garden existed in its present reconstructed condition for only a matter of a few years.[22] Changes occurred rapidly, and the garden evolved. Thus, this 'time capsual' represents only a fleeting reality – something that was once new and sensational, but also something that, in the twinkling of an eye, became past with the passing of a generation. Moreover, it was once part of a larger whole – a huge complex of parterres and wilderness that also existed in their brand-new condition for only a decade or two, and perhaps rather imperfectly. Their later evolution is every bit as much the story of gardening at Hampton Court, but a story that has to be edited out, if reconstruction is the overriding concern.

Thus, the philosophy of reconstruction for the Privy Garden should imply the further scientific reconstruction of the entire site to a notional date in the early eighteenth century. Indeed it should imply the elimination of the adjacent gardens in their current condition. Fancifully reconstructed in the 1920s and much-loved for the bright displays of flowers, these self-contained gardens would need to be destroyed if the whole complex were to achieve an appropriate degree of congruity.[23] Whether this is sustainable, both as an intellectual idea and as a commitment to maintenance of arrested growth around permanent horticultural renewal, seems to me open to debate. Beyond this too are other questions for the future: what level of public commitment is required to sustain these costly horticultural effects over time; and does charging for private access destroy the original quality of free public enjoyment?

2 Philosophical and practical implications

This brings me to the second part of this contribution: the philosophical and practical implications of such radical intervention. In the first place, I wish to mention a range of issues that the National Park Service in the United States has attempted to tackle in their guidelines for conservation philosophy, strategy and treatment.[24] When assessing a site, they are not merely concerned with thorough historical and archaeological research. Such site analysis is only a first step to determining an overall approach to the garden's conservation. There should be no prior assumption that radical restoration as opposed to cautious conservation will necessarily be the outcome of that analysis; but once an outcome has been determined, consistency of approach is essential. In the case of Hampton Court, therefore, the US National Park Service would leave little room for ambiguity over the long-term purpose of the conservation strategy. This clearly has advantages as a philosophical system; for each decision can be checked against the overall purpose of the undertaking. However, such laudable theory does not allow for the fact that political necessities sometimes require a discreet and piecemeal approach, or the fact that pragmatic concerns may not always fit neatly into the preconceived agenda.

'ORIGINAL FABRIC'   In this process of analysis, protecting the 'original fabric' and maintaining the overlays of planting are clearly a vital starting-point. This makes for good conservation and leads to the idea of conserving the garden, like the architecture, up to the point of the 'last significant change'.[25] It avoids rewriting the history of the site. Such issues are bound up with the question of preserving the historical integrity of the ensemble, and avoiding the creation of anachronisms or incongruities. For example, if it becomes necessary in a reconstruction to a specific period to invent things that never existed in actual historical time or to create forms that never coexisted in the past, then

11 The *plate-bande* of the parterre at Het Loo in 1991. (Photo: Mark Laird)

the curator of that site should be concerned. This is not protection and repair; this is fabrication. Indeed, it may be preferable to add a new layer to that site rather than to promote a false illusion of authenticity by masquerading under the label of 'original layout' or 'original planting'. In the meantime, checking the feasibility of care and upkeep over time, and ensuring objective interpretation (as opposed to facile publicity) – all these things may militate against radical intervention. In other words, whether wholesale restoration to one period is both desirable and sustainable will depend on many factors beyond the comprehensiveness of the archives and the completeness of the site evidence (which are clearly essential prerequisites for restoration).

Thus, before intervention of any kind is considered, the following factors should be carefully weighed up:
- What will have to be destroyed to realize the restoration and is that destruction acceptable or responsible? Is it possible to leave parts of the site for future investigation?
- What degree of reconstruction (as opposed to repair and restoration) will be required? And how accurate can that reconstruction be?
- What level of conjecture will be needed to complete the restoration/reconstruction and how can conjectural aspects be handled and interpreted?

12

- What are the implications of the restoration/reconstruction for upkeep and long-term maintenance? What degree of change and growth is permitted within a restoration strategy?
- What support will the restoration/reconstruction receive from the public, both immediately and in the longer term?

Only when all these factors conspire to suggest a positive outcome – when the level of archival and archaeological information is likely to be very high, and when the level of destruction of original fabric is likely to be very low – should the assessment of a strategy lead automatically in the direction of reconstruction or restoration. At this point, the discussion will have to include the analysis of horticultural practice from the period of the original design – usually the most elusive element, because archaeology can only locate limited bits of information. Archaeobotany has yet to prove, for example, exactly what was growing in a *plate-bande*, and in what configuration.[26] A great deal of contextual study will be required in order to restore the planted areas of a seventeenth- or eighteenth-century site with any degree of accuracy.

Such research goes beyond plant lists and planting systems to consider issues of colour composition, annual or cyclical alterations, techniques of 'forcing' and 'plunging', as well as short-term and long-term maintenance pro-

12 The reconstructed parterre of the Privy Garden at Hampton Court in 1995. (Photo: Mark Laird)
13 Detail of a newly replanted *plate-bande* in the Privy Garden at Hampton Court in 1995. (Photo: Mark Laird)

cedures.²⁷ Substantial progress should be made on these aspects of research before a decision is taken on the overall approach to conservation. If, after intensive studies, much remains purely speculative, the replanting will be more of an 'invention' than a 'restoration'. In certain circumstances this 'conjectural replanting' may be acceptable – the flower border is, after all, usually reversible – but that decision should come ahead of restoration, not as an afterthought.²⁸ Replanting thus forms part of an overall conservation strategy – a strategy in which the dangers of destroying 'original fabric', from whatever period, are weighed up scientifically against the gains of revitalizing the 'original design intent' of that one period when the garden is deemed to have been at its zenith.

ALTERNATIVE STRATEGIES   In almost all other circumstances when historical data are patchy or when later overlays are rich, alternative strategies are to be considered first. Here I should like to conclude with some thoughts on the options available to the responsible curator. In the first place, the analysis of site evidence offers the greatest potential for improved results. Today, a team of experts – the landscape architect, historian, planting historian, archaeologist, archaeobotanist, horticulturist, etc., all working together on an integrated

14

brief – is able to analyse a site with a degree of precision that was unthinkable twenty years ago.[29]

There have been considerable advances in the application and technology of garden archaeology. In particular, improved techniques have allowed us to verify details of a layout, including even the locations and dimensions of planted areas such as the *plate-bande*. The non-destructive technology of garden archaeology has proved very effective, and there seems every reason to believe that in another twenty years, a site might be analysed with minimal digging.[30] Just as the technology of medicine has allowed for non-intrusive diagnosis and treatment, so the technology of geophysical survey may eventually avoid the need for much destructive archaeology. The analysis of surviving vegetation awaits a similar scientific revolution. Thus, there is a strong argument for exploring the potential of non-destructive archaeology today; and thereafter, for adopting a strategy that maximizes protection of the site both above and below ground for future analysis.

Whether the principle of protection applied in a limited way at Tredegar House could be extended to cover a larger and more complex site – or to justify a new layer on top of the old – perhaps deserves investigation. Certainly, the opportunity to create an entirely new layout, perhaps inspired but not con-

14 The conjecturally reconstructed parterre at Tredegar House in 1993. (Photo: Mark Laird)

15 The parterre at Kirby Hall – a transposition of the contemporary grass parterre of Longleat in 1995. (Photo: Mark Laird)

strained by earlier ones, and free from concerns about archaeological fabric, offers an attractive option. This is especially true at a time when the imaginative licence of the 1970s and 1980s is increasingly dismissed and when a philosophy of 'minimal intervention' seems in danger of paralysing any radical action. However, the scope for such intervention is surely limited; it may protect archaeological evidence but it fails to protect the quality of repose that comes with age. What should be avoided at all costs is a twentieth-century version of a baroque parterre, using parts of the original fabric but otherwise inventing the decorative finish. Many of the projects of the 1970s and early 1980s were based on this formula, and there is no reason to return to their methods. The reconstruction of the Privy Garden at Hampton Court has set up a standard for the 1990s that should be emulated or surpassed. Nevertheless, as I have tried to illustrate, even such meticulous reconstruction poses huge dilemmas. Furthermore, since the vast majority of sites do not allow for such intensive scrutiny, this is not usually an option. Most curators should be primarily concerned to uphold the overriding principles of conservation: the protection, recording and repair of original fabric. The appropriate place for exploring reconstruction – with all its speculative difficulties – is surely on paper and not as a laboratory experiment on a living site.[31]

1 For the definition of terms such as 'original fabric', see Laird, '«Conjectural Replanting»', p.320, and Laird, 'Guidelines 1'. David Jacques uses the terms 'original fabric' and 'authentic fabric' in 'A Practical Philosophy', pp.122-23.
2 A wider discussion of these issues is provided by Laird, '«Conjectural Replanting»', pp.320-43, and Schmidt, 'Spezifische Probleme', pp.283-92.
3 Laird, '«Conjectural Replanting»', passim.
4 Discussed further in ibid., especially p.321, and in Jacques, 'Historical Aims' and 'A Practical Philosophy'.
5 See Laird, 'Restoration of Planting', pp.132-41.
6 See Harvey, *Restoring Period Gardens*, p.40.
7 See Goulty, *Heritage Gardens*, pp.63-66.
8 Harvey, *Restoring Period Gardens*, p.44.
9 See the contributions by Laird and Woudstra to the National Trust internal report on Ham House of 1993.
10 Elfgang, 'The Pomeranzengarten in Leonberg', pp.175-82.
11 Harvey, *Restoring Period Gardens*, p.46; National Trust Guidebook, *Westbury Court Garden*, pp.10-12, 14-15, 18-20, 41-44.
12 Hansmann, 'Parterres', pp.165-69, and Wertz, 'Wiederherstellung', pp.198-204.
13 Laird and Harvey, '«A Cloth of Tissue»', p.161.
14 Ibid., pp.172-73.
15 Goulty, *Heritage Gardens*, pp.115-18, and Hansmann, 'Parterres', p.168.
16 See Barkhof and Oldenburger-Ebbers, 'Plants for the Restoration', and the special issue of *Groen*, June 1984, which is dedicated to the reconstruction of Het Loo.
17 Woudstra, 'The Planting', pp.43-77.
18 Dix and Parry, 'The Excavation', pp.79-118.
19 Harvey, *Restoring Period Gardens*, p.46.
20 Ibid., p.59.
21 Ibid., p.44, and Dix, 'Kirby Hall and Hampton Court'.
22 Jacques, 'The History', pp.23-42.
23 The ideas of 'congruity' and 'integrity' are discussed in Laird, '«Conjectural Replanting»', pp.322-24.
24 See the National Park Service, 'Guidelines for the Treatment of Historic Landscapes'.
25 The term 'last significant change' was first used by David Jacques at English Heritage, 'Historical Aims'. See also Laird, '«Conjectural Replanting»', p.322.
26 De Moulins and Weir, 'Environmental Techniques in Gardens'.

27 Examples of such research are provided by Laird, '«Our Equally Favorite Hobby Horse»', Laird and Harvey, '«A Cloth of Tissue»', MacDougall, 'A Cardinal's Bulb Garden', and Woudstra, 'The Planting'.
28 See Laird, '«Conjectural Replanting»', pp. 339-40.
29 See Woudstra, 'The Planting', pp. 49-50, and Dix and Parry, 'The Excavation', passim.
30 Linford, 'Non Destructive Techniques', and Dix and Parry, 'The Excavation', p. 101 and fig. 106.
31 See again Laird, '«Conjectural Replanting»', pp. 339-40.

Barkhof, H.R., and C.S. Oldenburger-Ebbers. 'Plants for the Restoration of the Baroque Garden of the Palace of the Loo at Apeldoorn'. In *Journal of Garden History*, 1 (1981), 4, pp. 293-304. See also the guidebook to Het Loo and the special issue of *Groen* (June 1984).

De Moulins, Dominique, and David A. Weir. 'The Potential and Use of Environmental Techniques in Gardens'. Paper presented at the garden archaeology conference at Strawberry Hill, June 1995, and published in *Journal of Garden History*, 17 (1997), 1, pp. 40-47.

Dix, Brian, and Stephen Parry. 'The Excavation of the Privy Garden'. In Simon Thurley (ed.), *The King's Privy Garden at Hampton Court Palace 1689-1995*. London, 1995, pp. 79-118.

Dix, B. 'Kirby Hall & Hampton Court, two UK Restoration Projects'. Paper presented at the garden archaeology conference at Strawberry Hill, June 1995, and published as '«Diging of Borders»: Reflections on Archaeology and Garden Restoration', in *Journal of Garden History*, 17 (1997), 1, pp. 11-18.

Elfgang, Alfons. 'Historically Correct Reconstruction Does Not Conflict with Present Day Recreation Requirements – Example: The Pomeranzengarten in Leonberg'. In *Garten und Landschaft*, 3 (1981), pp. 175-82.

Goulty, Sheena Mackellar. *Heritage Gardens: Care, Conservation and Management*. London and New York, 1993.

Hansmann, Wilfried. 'Parterres: Entwicklung, Typen, Elemente'. In Dieter Hennebo (ed.), *Gartendenkmalpflege: Grundlagen der Erhaltung Historischer Gärten und Grünanlagen*, Stuttgart, 1985.

Harvey, John. *Restoring Period Gardens* (2nd ed.). Princes Risborough, 1993.

Jacques, David. 'Gartendenkmalpflegerische Positionen und Prinzipien im Vereinigten Königreich von Großbritannien'. In *Die Gartenkunst*, 1 (1991), pp. 131-43.

Jacques, D. 'A Practical Philosophy for Assisting Parks and Gardens'. In *Restoration '92*. London, 1992, pp. 119-23.

Jacques, D.L. 'Historical Aims in the Treatment of Parks and Gardens'. Unpublished report for English Heritage, draft of 7 August 1992.

Jacques, D. 'The History of the Privy Garden'. In Simon Thurley (ed.), *The King's Privy Garden at Hampton Court Palace 1689-1995*. London, 1995.

Laird, Mark. '«Conjectural Replanting». Leitlinien zur Widerbepflanzung historischer Gärten aufgrund von Analogieschlüssen'. In *Die Gartenkunst*, 2 (1994), pp. 320-43.

Laird, M. 'Restoration of Planting in Eighteenth Century Landscape Gardens'. In *Restoration '92*. London, 1992, pp. 132-41.

Laird, M. 'Guidelines for Conjectural Replanting' I & II. Unpublished reports for English Heritage, 1993 and 1994.

Laird, M. '«Our Equally Favorite Hobby Horse»: The Flower Gardens of Lady Elizabeth Lee at Hartwell and the 2nd Earl Harcourt at Nuneham Courtenay'. In *Garden History*, 18/2 (1990), pp. 103-54 (including appendix by John H. Harvey).

Laird, M., and J.H. Harvey. '«A Cloth of Tissue of Divers Colours»: The English Flower Border, 1660-1735'. In *Garden History*, 21/2 (1993), pp. 158-205.

Linford, Neil. 'Non Destructive Techniques in English Gardens'. Paper presented at the garden archaeology conference at Strawberry Hill, June 1995, and published by Mark A. Cole, Andrew E.U. David, Neil T. Linford, Paul K. Linford and Andrew W. Payne as 'Non Destructive Techniques in English Gardens: Geophysical Prospecting', in *Journal of Garden History*, 17 (1997), 1, pp. 26-40.

MacDougall, Elisabeth Blair. 'A Cardinal's Bulb Garden'. In *Fountains, Statues, and Flowers: Studies in Italian Gardens of the Sixteenth and Seventeenth Centuries*. Washington, DC, 1994.

Schmidt, Erika. 'Spezifische Probleme der Erhaltung von Gartendenkmalen'. In *Die Gartenkunst*, 2 (1993), pp. 283-92.

Wertz, Hubert Wolfgang. 'Widerherstellung und Unterhaltung von Parterreanlagen dargestellt am Beispiel des Schwetzinger Parterres'. In Dieter Hennebo (ed.), *Gartendenkmalpflege: Grundlagen der Erhaltung Historischer Gärten und Grünanlagen*. Stuttgart, 1985.

Woudstra, Jan. 'The Planting of the Privy Garden'. In Simon Thurley (ed.), *The King's Privy Garden at Hampton Court Palace 1689-1995*. London, 1995, pp. 43-77.

P.-A. Lablaude   *The Park of Versailles*

The Park of Versailles.
Projects and achievements
PIERRE-ANDRÉ LABLAUDE

THE DOMAIN OF THE PARK OF VERSAILLES   The aim of this paper is not to give a detailed history of the creation of the Park of Versailles. Rather, it wants to draw attention to the problems raised by the archaeological possibilities, landscaping options and technical alternatives which confront those who today are responsible for the conservation and restoration of this site.

Under Louis XIV, the Park of Versailles comprised three concentric enclosures (fig. 1):
- the 'Gardens' themselves (approximately 90 hectares)
- the 'Small Park', originally extending over 1,700 hectares
- the 'Great Park', which at one time was a hunting park of 6,000 hectares, surrounded by 43 kilometres of walls, and which has totally disappeared today, since it was divided at the time of the Revolution and urbanized during the nineteenth and twentieth centuries.

The present park, which is owned by the State as heir to the wealth of the Crown, is reduced to the 90 hectares of gardens and the Small Park, which has seen its area reduced to 600 hectares. Nevertheless, the site remains an area of remarkable dimensions and we can quote the following figures as an illustration: there are 132 kilometres of rows of trees, 12 kilometres of *charmilles* (hedges of hornbeam) and 12 hectares of ornamental lakes and pools.

It is mainly the problems associated with the restoration of the gardens in the immediate proximity of the Château which will be discussed below.

PRINCIPLES OF DESIGN   The first hunting pavilion, as constructed under Louis XIII, was accompanied by a first garden, created by Jacques de Menours and Jacques Boyceau; it was rearranged in 1639 by the landscape architect Claude Mollet. The first work on the park, undertaken by Louis XIV, was begun in 1662 under the direction of Le Nôtre and progressed over the next fifty years simultaneously with the gradual extensions of the Château (fig. 2). Of course,

1 Plan of the Petit Parc de Versailles, by Le Pautre, 1710. Musée de Versailles

Le Nôtre was not the inventor of the French-style garden; he pursued an old tradition which dated back to the end of the Renaissance, and which through the years established the principles followed in such a spectacular way at Versailles. What are those principles behind the garden's composition and how have they been applied at Versailles?

They are, first of all, the principles of a symmetric composition based on a series of axes, in this case a main axis over five kilometres long which starts in the east, where the town lies, crosses the forecourt, the Château itself from the King's Bedchamber to the Galerie des Glaces, the parterres or flowers-beds, the Tapis Vert, the Bassin d'Apollon and the Grand Canal, until it disappears beyond the horizon in the west (fig. 2). This main axis is accompanied by parallel secondary axes, such as the Allées des Saisons, as well as axes perpendicular to it, which define the square-grid pattern of the gardens.

The second principle of the composition concerns the truly dramatic way in which the sloping site has been formed into terraces (fig. 3). The present park extends over an area which indeed is largely artificial. The ancient village of Versailles lay in a marshy valley which was the source of a small brook, the Rû de Gally.

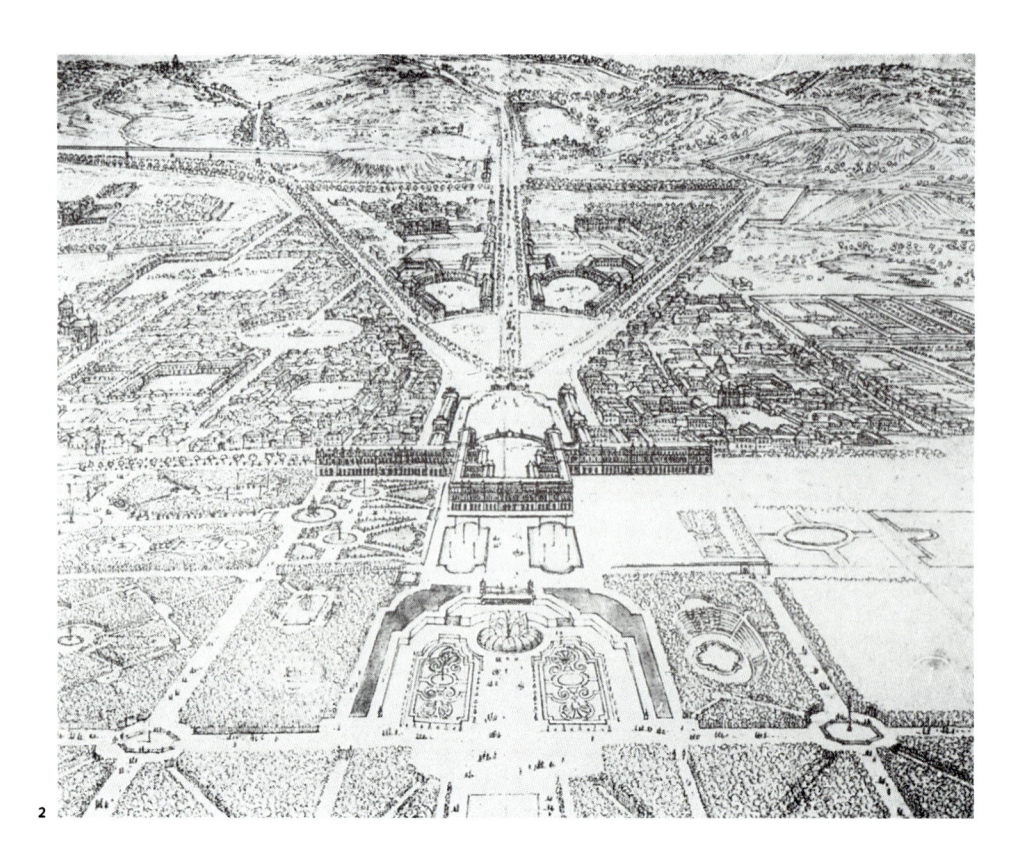

It took thousands of workmen many years to reconstruct the site. An entire hillside was levelled to allow the passage of the Avenue de Paris, and the resulting spoil was reused to make up the terraces and ramps which formed the base of the Château and the gardens. They looked out over the descending perspective of three platforms:

- the first and uppermost towards the west, comprising the Parterre de Latone, the Tapis Vert and the Grand Canal (fig. 3)
- the second towards the south, comprising the Parterre du Midi, the Orangery and the Pièce d'Eau des Suisses (fig. 4)
- the third towards the north, comprising the Parterres du Nord, the Bosquets du Nord (Northern Groves) and the Bassin de Neptune.

The third principle employed at the origin of Versailles is that of stepped vegetation, in accordance with the hierarchy of the various landscape strata, so that away from the Château, one passes gradually from an extremely rich architecture towards more natural surroundings (fig. 3). Thus, Versailles follows the classical hierarchy of the French garden:

- box-hedged decorated parterres, as close as possible to the Château in such a way that they may be seen from the upper floors of the building as a rolled-out

3

2 Bird's-eye view of the gardens, the castle and the city of Versailles, by Israël Silvestre, c.1684.

Musée du Louvre, Paris. Cabinet des Dessins

3 The Parterre d'Eau and the great west axis of the Allée du Tapis Vert. (Photo: P.-A. Lablaude)

carpet beneath the windows, and also including flower-beds whose scent will pervade the rooms through the open windows of the ground floor (fig. 4)
- groves and avenues composed as architectural vegetation, occupying the middle ground of the garden, pruned to mark out the pathways but also, during the first phase, cropped so as to allow a view of the countryside beyond
- finally, impressive woodland perspectives on the horizon, the rows of trees closest to the Château partly pruned, those to the lateral and distant perspectives left untouched.

With respect to these 'classical' principles of the French garden, Versailles distinguishes itself by a number of elaborate details, such as the ornamental basins and the interior arrangement of the groves.

In a classical garden, water is naturally confined to the lower parts of the site; in the case of Versailles, these are, for instance, the Bassin de Neptune, the Bassin d'Apollon and the Grand Canal, which ensure the drainage of the former marshland. This called for extremely costly refinements, which could only be installed thanks to the technical skill of the Frères Francini. They belonged to a family of Italian fountain builders who came to France at the beginning of the seventeenth century with Queen Maria de' Medicis. The water was introduced at the summit of an artificial mound in the form of two very delicate *parterres d'eau* ('water-beds') which, situated on the highest terrace, reflect the sun, the sky and the passing clouds like two mirrors (fig. 3).

4

LE NÔTRE'S DESIGN AS SEEN TODAY   To what extent does the Park of Versailles correspond today to the image conceived by its creators? To what extent does it correspond to the glory they beheld in the year 1700?

While the main axes of its composition, the layout, the stepped hillside terraces and the colourful richness of the flower-beds have all been preserved, the earliest elements of the architectural and natural composition, the bosquets, have been the subject of serious neglect, both of the botanical parts – alignment, internal harmony – and of their architecture and decoration: basins, fountains, flower-beds, trellis-work, statues and sculptures.

A garden is not just a work of art, it is also a work of art in perpetual transformation by the natural phenomenon of vegetal growth. The borders which marked the perimeters of the groves during the reign of Louis XIV took three different forms, depending on their positions:

- that of a simple low trellis fence, of about two metres high; overhead, the internal branch structure was pruned vertically by simply lopping off the encroaching branches
- that of a screen of *charmilles* pruned vertically, their crowns lopped-off at a height of about seven metres (fig. 5)
- that of a third variation, combining the two preceding methods so as to form a border consisting of perimeter *charmilles*, sidewalk and trellis fence.

However, in the course of time, the trees planted inside the groves became

5

4 The Parterre du Midi. (Photo: P.-A. Lablaude)

5 The Bassin de Flore and the green palisades of the Allées des Saisons. Engraving from the Album Vanheck, 1716. Service d'Architecture du Domaine de Versailles

too high to allow pruning by ladder. They hung over the pathways, putting the *charmilles* in the shade and tending to suffocate them. So, in less than a century the classical image of strictly pruned groves surrounded by tall hedges gave way to the romantic image of low belts of hornbeams overtopped by high clumps of free-standing trees (fig. 6).

In 1776 Louis XVI decided to fell all the trees in the gardens and the park and have these replanted, not along the lines of the new romantic English model – as was the fashion at the end of the eighteenth century – but by faithfully retaining the layout adopted by his ancestor, Louis XIV. This episode was depicted in two famous paintings by Hubert Robert (fig. 7).

Gradually, the newly planted trees reached maturity, and a little over a century later, between 1860 and 1880 in the days of the Second Empire, the gardens and the park were again completely replanted.

Thus we see that, in the history of the Park of Versailles, the gardens have been replanted every century: in 1675, 1775 and 1875. On the strength of this hundred-year cycle, replanting is now overdue by more than twenty years.

Why, then, has it not yet been carried out? Without doubt, it is in the first place for financial reasons. But another reason may be that today, in an environment so highly urbanized and in a context of ecological reaction to the demands

6

of an industrialized society, artists and intellectuals as well as the public at large have grown accustomed and, little by little, attached to this romantic image of the park. A bit melancholy, sad even, with its big trees overhanging the alleys and shading the moss-covered statues, it creates a special atmosphere, yet is far from that brilliant composition originally imagined by Le Nôtre. And perhaps it is also because no one has the courage to face the protests of the press which a major tree felling is bound to arouse.

REPLANTING THE GARDENS   The inevitable decision has therefore been postponed year after year. However, the gale of 2 February 1990 took that decision off our hands (fig. 8). In little more than one night, it felled well over 1,300 trees in the gardens and the park, causing considerable damage to the decoration.

Since then, a great number of trees are severely damaged, many of them unstable or exposed 'in the front line', due to the disappearance of those trees which used to offer shelter from the wind. So today the park finds itself at the mercy of new storms, with all the risks of jeopardizing garden decor (statues, vases, benches, trellis fences) as well as visitors.

Consequently, the questions which arise today concerning the replanting of the gardens are the following:
· Should we replant with the eventual aim to restore the gardens to their state at the time of Louis XVI, that is, similar to the state they are in now, with low peripheral hedges and high clumps of trees? In effect, this constitutes the last-known historic state
· Or should we seek to return to the times of Louis XIV, when the gardens had seven-metre-high palisades and low copses? This seems to be the more satisfactory choice, as it is consistent with the image of Versailles created by Louis XIV.

As we have seen, the original vegetal composition was laid out in such a way that it progressively grew in space and height in relation to the distance from the Château:
· the 'water-beds' at ground level, close to the Château
· the beds of box and flowers approximately sixty centimetres high above the soil
· next, the groves, up to a height of a little over twelve metres
· finally, on the horizon, trees of natural growth reaching a height of more than thirty metres.

The present groves with trees reaching forty metres completely disturb the balance of the composition; they shorten the perspective by forming a screen which blocks the view into the distance and blurs the observation of the main

6   The Bassin de Neptune and the Bosquets du Nord, seventy years after their planting. Drawing attributed to Portail, mid-eighteenth century. Musée de Versailles

7

axes. If we replant today to restore the situation as it was in the seventeenth century, what types of tree should we use? Then, elms were used, a solution denied to us today because of Dutch elm disease. In the eighteenth century, oaks; in the nineteenth century, a mixture of elms, plane-trees and horse chestnuts. Since the beginning of our century, replanting has been done mostly with lime-trees.

HISTORICAL STUDIES   The first study dates from 1990, when the northern groves were examined for the first time. The aim was to identify the species that would provide an overall stabilizing effect on the vegetal composition, as close as possible to that of the gardens in the eighteenth century and on the basis of the many contemporary pictures of Versailles at our disposal.

While the reconstruction of screens of *charmilles* to a height slightly in excess of seven metres (which corresponds to the use of a twenty-foot ladder for traditional pruning, as at Versailles) does not pose any technical problems, the situation is rather more complex as far as the internal planting of the groves is concerned. We must bear in mind that the choice of a species of big high-growing trees – such as oaks, beeches, plane-trees, limes or horse chestnuts, as used in previous centuries – would indeed repeat the process and eventually lead to trees of the disastrous height of forty metres.

The decision was therefore made to establish a natural ceiling of vegetation equivalent to the level of growth of the ancient woodland as shown by illustrations from the turn of the seventeenth century. The growth should not exceed an average height, which Dezaillier d'Argenville, in his work on the internal plantation of groves, fixed at an ideal level of forty feet (just over twelve metres).

To achieve this, we must restrict ourselves to the use of less noble trees by choosing a species of average development. Moreover, in order to obtain a satisfactory composition and a rapid repair of the trauma incurred by the felling of trees, we should look for fast-growing trees. The following are some of the species that have been chosen:

- maple (*Acer negundo* or *Acer campestre*)
- alder (*Alnus incana*, *Alnus cordata* or *Alnus glutinosa*)
- common hornbeam (*Carpinus betulus* or *Ostrya Carpinifolia*)
- sweet chestnut (*Castania sativa*)
- walnut (*Juglans regia*)
- hazel (*Corylus colurna*)
- service tree (*Sorbus domestica*).

7 The gardens of Versailles during the felling of trees in the winter of 1774-75 in the Bosquet d'Apollon. Painting by Hubert Robert. Musée de Versailles

8 Effects of the storm of February 2nd, 1990 in the bosquets of the gardens of Versailles. (Photo: J.C. Marty)

P.-A. Lablaude   *The Park of Versailles*

ARRANGEMENT OF THE GROVES   The second theme of restoration to be carried out in the gardens concerns the internal arrangement of the groves.

To give an impression of the richness of the groves, which has mostly disappeared today, here are some examples of what can only be described as outdoor salons which at one time adorned the gardens, such as the Bosquet des Dômes, created in 1675, which included two marble pavilions, both constructed in 1677 and destroyed in 1820. There was also the Bosquet de la Colonnade, built by Mansart in 1685 and remarkable for the impressive contrast between the white Carrara marble and the multicoloured red, blue and violet marble of French origin. Les Trois Fontaines was a bosquet with a grove of trees and shrubs and without any architectural or sculptural adornment, simply embellished with three basins and quoted in various texts as having been drawn 'by the King's hand'. It was created by Le Nôtre in 1680 and was destroyed at the end of the eighteenth century; today its restoration is envisaged for the next five years. The Bosquet de l'Arc de Triomphe used to be the richest of all the groves at Versailles, with its profusion of multicoloured marble in the obelisk-shaped fountains and its triumphal arch of gold-leave wrought iron. It was built in 1677 and destroyed in 1801.

10

9 The Bosquet d'Encelade in its original state, with its trellis architecture and its eight fountains around the central basin. Painting by Cotelle, 1688/89. Musée de Versailles
10 The Bosquet d'Encelade in 1990, a result of the simplifications achieved in the beginning of the eighteenth century. (Photo: P.-A. Lablaude)

The Bosquet d'Encelade is the first grove to be restored as part of the programme of restoration, or rather reconstruction, at Versailles. It was created in 1676 by Le Nôtre and Lebrun, and is laid out around a statue of the giant Enceladus, a mythological figure who attempted to climb Mount Olympus and was crushed under the rocks (fig. 9). The statue is made of lead, formerly gilded, and has a characteristic lyrical and baroque expression (fig. 10). Enceladus suffers under heaps of stone while spouting a jet of water some twenty-three metres high in the air. Eight small fountains of natural sandstone on low platforms of grass accompany the central basin. The entire composition is surrounded by a high trellis 'arcade', notable for its pavilions in the form of triumphal arches sheltering small wooden benches for discrete conversation. It was covered by scented plants such as lilacs, honeysuckle and jasmine, and decorated with gilded metal vases and a topiary of yew trees trained and pruned in vessel-like shapes (fig. 9). Thus the gallery, with its charm and its rustic style, contrasted markedly with the statue of the dying giant and the mythological drama being enacted at the centre of the grove. All the peripheral decorations, platforms, fountains and trellis arcades were destroyed in 1708. The current reconstruction, which was begun in December 1994 and will be completed in

11

1997, aims at restoring the entire Bosquet d'Encelade to its original state of 1676. The work is carried out in many phases: survey of the site, archival research, excavations, analogical, chronological and technical studies and investigation into trellis construction, the making of a scale model and the construction of a prototypical trellis section, designed in accordance with the original principles, with an iron frame carrying the ornamental wooden trellis (fig. 11).

OPERATIONS IN PROGRESS   To give an idea of the multiplicity of the operations being carried out at present in the gardens and park of Versailles, let us in conclusion consider some of the other work in progress, for a better understanding of the wide range of procedures and practices.

Firstly, the conservation work itself, which aims at preserving the authentic material, as in the case of statuaries, or, as much as possible, in the case of architectural construction elements. Then, the restoration work, that is, the partial replacement of materials too much damaged to be preserved, while guaranteeing a strictly identical reproduction – as in the case of the recent restoration of the marble Mansart colonnade.

Next, the replacement of perishable objects; for instance, the complete

12

11 Prototype of one of the pavilions in the trellis gallery for the reconstruction of the Bosquet d'Encelade. (Photo: P.-A. Lablaude)

12 Restoration project for the Rondeau d'Apollon (detail), 1994. Drawing by P.-A. Lablaude

replanting of a row of trees along a path. Or the most ambitious operation of all: the reconstruction, on the basis of the archival or archaeological database, of former compositions that have disappeared. This is the case with the Rondeau d'Apollon which only three years ago was still planted with old plane-trees dating back to 1876. The original trees, however, were chestnuts alternating with topiaries. The refined art of topiary was one of the most remarkable characteristics of the Versailles of Louis XIV; it has now completely disappeared. That is why today it figures largely in our endeavours to restore Versailles to its original state (fig.12).

CONCLUSION   There are certain cases where the archives, the old drawings and archaeology are too inaccurate for us to attempt a truly authentic reconstruction, so that here we have to resort to our imagination.

The most characteristic example is that of the flower-beds of the Parterre de Trianon, the only parterre of which we possess a precise botanical inventory. This has allowed us to attempt a reconstruction of the flower-setting of the period (fig.13). The authenticity of these flower-beds is not, however, one hundred per cent, due to some botanical inaccuracies in the definition of species and also because of the disappearance of certain seventeenth-century botanical stocks. Moreover, the cost of maintenance of such a type of flower-bed

13

would be extremely high. In most such cases, therefore, we have to resort to our imagination, contenting ourselves with modern varieties of flowers to regain the colours and the layout of shades in the spirit of the compositions of former days.

In conclusion, the restoration of a historic garden inevitably involves a number of different operations – conservation, restoration, replacement, a faithful reconstruction or an imagined one. But while each of these operations aims at true authenticity, we must realize that we will never be completely satisfied; we can only try to get as close to the 'real thing' as possible. To my mind, this is the only way to let the amateur of historic gardens experience the sensation of travelling through time, and to make him feel the mystery and poetry of these gardens.

For further reading: P.-A. Lablaude, *Les jardins de Versailles*, Paris, 1995, and by the same author, 'Restauration et régénération de l'architecture végétale du jardin de Versailles', in *Monumental*, 04 (Direction du Patrimoine, 1993), pp. 76-85.

13 The parterres of the Jardin Français at the Trianon.
(Photo: P.-A. Lablaude)

J.Woudstra *The design of the Privy Garden at Hampton Court*

The design of the Privy Garden at Hampton Court

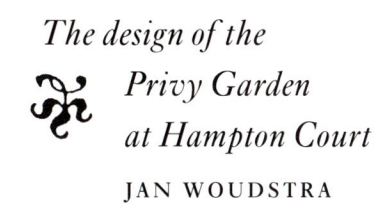

JAN WOUDSTRA

THE OPENING OF the reconstructed Privy Garden at Hampton Court in July 1995 marked the end of a project which had started in 1992 and strove towards the restoration of the design as it had been at the death of William III in 1702. It also marked the beginning of regular maintenance, which is one of the most crucial factors for the appearance of the design.

1 The Privy Garden

The Privy Garden – the monarch's private garden – was the area where the monarch could withdraw without being disturbed by courtiers and politicians (figs. 1, 2 and 3, 8 and 9). The Privy Garden at Hampton Court had been in existence since 1530, the reign of Henry VIII, but went through many changes in the course of the next generations. When William was invited jointly with Mary Stuart to accept the British throne in 1689, Hampton Court was chosen as their principal residence. However, the palace was considered out of date and plans were developed by a team of craftsmen lead by Sir Christopher Wren to rebuild substantial parts of it. The old state apartments were demolished and rebuilt. At the same time, Hans Willem Bentinck, William III's adviser on design matters in the Netherlands, was appointed Superintendent of Royal Gardens. For all practical purposes, most of the duties of this position were carried out by George London. The early projects included a new approach avenue from the north, and the Fountain Garden. The latter was made after designs by Daniel Marot, who had also worked on William's Dutch properties.

The new Privy Garden was laid out to the same width as the extended state apartments. These had been provided with an orangery on the ground floor for sheltering orange trees during the winter. The garden itself was laid out as a *gazon coupé*, or cutwork, surrounded with terraces. The soil of the former mound on which Henry VIII's banqueting house to the south had rested was

1 Leonard Knyff. *Sketch Depicting Hampton Court from the South.* Detail. c.1702. Pen and ink. The Trustees of the British Museum

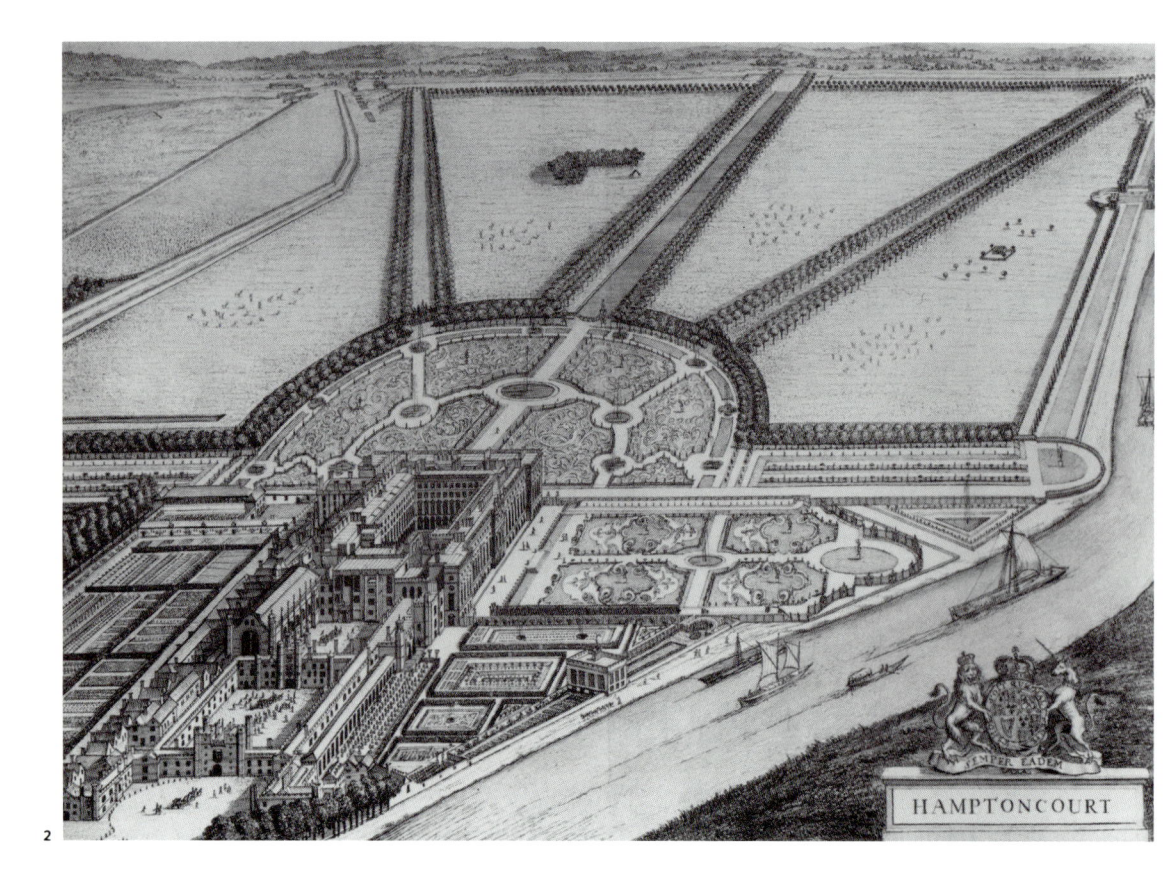

dispersed to provide a view. Unfortunately, it was impossible to see the Thames from the palace, and this was the reason for the subsequent alterations from 1699 to 1701/2. These changes took place in a rather *ad hoc* manner in three stages. The first stage, carried out by Bentinck in 1699, comprised the widening of the central path and laying out new borders. The second stage included a reduction of levels in the garden and the removal of the remains of the former mound as well as the replanting of the garden. While this provided a more open view, the Thames remained invisible, and the King asked for new designs. Subsequently, a painted wooden model of the garden was produced. He also asked for a mock-up of *repoussé* ironwork screens to be set up. These were designed by Jean Tijou (fl. 1680s-1710s), a Frenchman who came to England drawn by the promise of lucrative contracts. In the end, it was decided that the levels of the garden were to be reduced even further in order to provide a sight-line through to the Thames. The newly planted garden was dug up, and the new design executed. Whereas the work in the gardens was carried out by Henry Wise, it is not known who designed them. It may have been Marot, though many of the stylistic elements can also be found in the work of Wise's partner, George London. London and Wise were the royal gardeners about the turn of the seventeenth century. As joint partners they were also responsible for the largest contemporary English nursery, the Brompton nursery, and for the design and layout of many of the most important gardens of the period.

William did not live to enjoy the completed design; his horse stumbled in the park, the King fell off and died some time later. After his death, Queen Anne cut down the maintenance costs of the gardens, which were also simplified in places. The Court did not assemble at Hampton Court any more after 1737 and the management was changed accordingly. Capability Brown, who was royal gardener at Hampton Court from 1764 to 1783, put an end to the clipping of shaped trees, with the result that the trees outgrew their former proportions. Subsequent generations planted new trees between the old ones, which gradually obstructed the view of the Thames. The restoration of the King's apartments after the great fire of 1986 led to a reassessment of the relationship between the palace and the landscape, and resulted in a reconstruction of the layout of 1702.

After Bentinck's resignation in 1699, a comprehensive record has been kept of the 1699-1702 alterations. Bentinck's position had become redundant, and the Office of Works was given the day-to-day responsibility for the

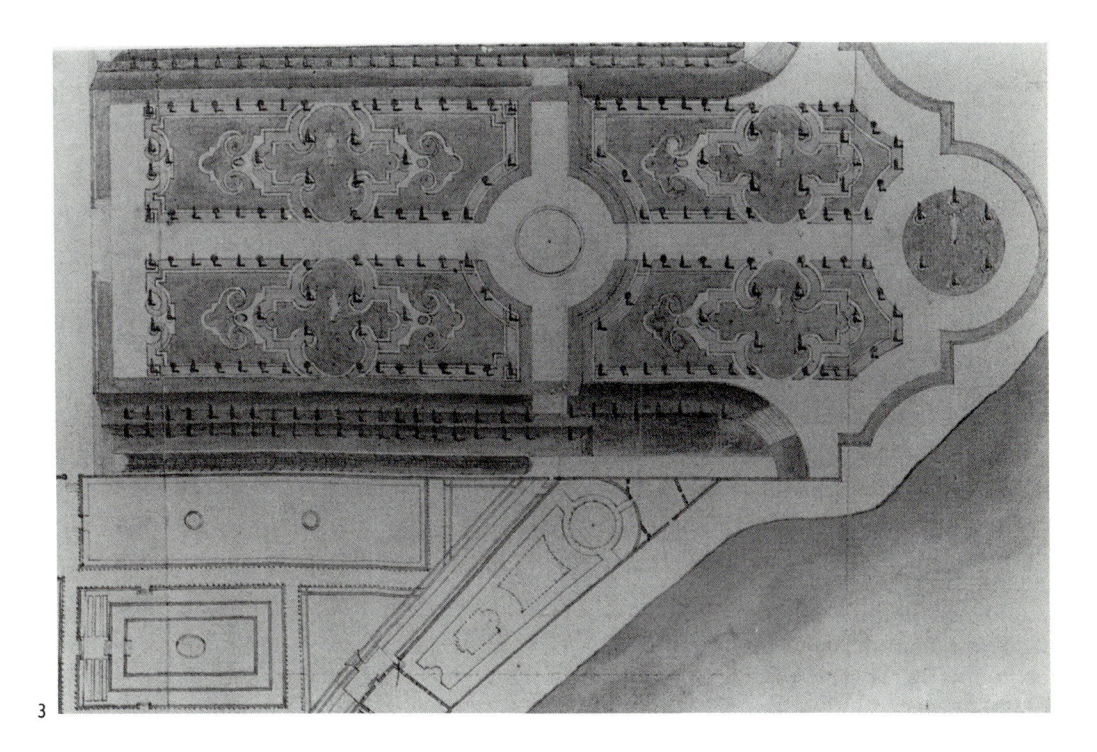

3

2 Leonard Knyff, Johannes Kip. Bird's-Eye View of Hampton Court Palace at the Time of the Death of William III. c. 1703. Engraving. The Trustees of the British Museum.
3 Anonymous. Plan of the Privy Garden on a Plan of Hampton Court. 1710-13. The Trustees of the Sir John Soane Museum.

changes. Their records, referred to as the WORK Accounts, now at the Public Record Office in Kew, made possible a detailed analysis of the construction of the garden. A series of plans revealed details of its layout. Moreover, the way the original garden had been made ensured that good archaeological evidence became available as the team of archaeologists completed their two-year programme.

This paper deals with the landscaping materials used by Henry Wise, the gardener in charge, in the Privy Garden layout of 1701/2, both soft and hard. It does not deal with materials that have been removed, stonework and statuary, since these were supplied by others. The bower, however, is included, even though it dates from before the layout of 1689.

GRAVEL Contrary to continental practice, English gardeners liked to use gravels which contained clay and could be rolled to a hard smooth surface (fig. 5). The general practice at Hampton Court was to lay the walks with six inches of coarse gravel, covered by six inches of screened gravel. Surviving samples demonstrate that the early-eighteenth-century gravel was a screened Thames gravel of $\tfrac{3}{4}$ inches down to dust. The records show that the gravel at

4

Hampton Court originated mainly from a pit in the park and one in Hampton Court Green, while the gravel in the Privy Garden probably came from the site itself. Archaeological survey found that the walks had a camber and a shallow gutter which led the excess water into a sophisticated drainage system. Portland stone rollers were used to keep the gravel firm, and rolling, probably in line with contemporary practice, took place on a daily basis. For the reconstructed walks, a gravel from a pit in nearby Romsey was used, with a slightly higher clay content than the original Thames gravel; it was chosen because of its ease of maintenance.

SAND   Sand was frequently used in English parterres to accentuate various figurative forms in the design (fig. 4). It was applied in strips referred to as 'alleys'. In the Privy Garden, local yellow river sand originating from a pit in the park was used. Elsewhere, the sand was laid six inches thick, and archival research came up with an inexplicably large quantity which would have allowed a thickness of 18 inches – which, however, is unlikely and is not borne out by archaeological findings. The maintenance of the sand strip would have included regular raking, and an occasional weeding.

5

4 Sand was applied in narrow 'alleys' along the *plates-bandes* and in the *gazon coupé*. (Photo: Jan Woudstra)

5 Unlike eighteenth-century practice, when the gravel walks were laid with manual labour, the walks were relaid with modern machinery (spring 1995). (Photo: Jan Woudstra)

BLACK EARTH FOR THE BORDERS   The records show that the borders had been filled with black earth, which was enriched with well-rotted manure and dug over three times. The team of archaeologists discovered that the borders were backfilled with a combination of soils which for the most part comprised a dark-brown sandy loam sandwiched between two red loams. The dark-brown soil was found to have been deliberately enriched. Microfabric analysis showed that it contained sieved building rubble and domestic waste, including bones and ashes. The soil was further enriched with organic material including bracken (*Pteridium aquilinum* [L.] Kuhn). While the organic material ensured a supply of nutrients and retention of water, the less enriched layer on the top prevented the plant roots from being scorched by direct contact with any fresh organic material. The borders were usually laid with a 'carp's back', that is, higher at the centre than at the sides. This arrangement saw to it that the plants would be set off. Contemporary authors suggest that borders should be raised about six inches in the middle.

The archaeologists found that the early-eighteenth-century border trenches were about three feet deep. However, multiplication of the total length of border by its width suggests a much larger quantity of black earth, allowing a depth of five feet. The discrepancy may partly be explained by the fact that, instead of following the design, the trenches were much wider in places; for example, at

6

the north end the trench was 17 feet wide instead of six feet, which required a much larger quantity of soil to fill in the whole border.

EARTH UNDERNEATH TURF   The records also show the use of loamy earth underneath turf, which varied in thickness from five inches in the parterres to almost eight inches on the terraces (fig. 7). This was confirmed by the archaeologists, who found that the maximum amount of earth on the parterre area was eight inches. The fairly poor loamy soil would have provided the right substrate for the acidic turf planted on top of it.

TURF   The treatment of good turf in the seventeenth century was considered to be typically English, and keeping turf 'after the English manner' was a well-known saying. The finest turf for use in gardens was that on which sheep normally grazed; it was weed-free but contained camomile. Maintenance included frequent rolling, first with a wooden roller to remove the worm casts and afterwards with a stone roller. Grass was to be mown at least twice a week. The largest area in the Privy Garden was covered with grass. The turf for the Privy Garden probably originated from nearby Molesey Hurst, a lowland heath with acidic soils. The composition of this turf has been determined from what would have occurred in this habitat. The garden was relaid with turf grown

7

6 Turf was an important component in the design of the Privy Garden. It was raised especially for the reconstructed garden (spring 1995). (Photo: Jan Woudstra)

7 Archaeology had revealed the thickness of the layers of earth underneath the turf, and this was faithfully reconstructed (autumn 1994). (Photo: Jan Woudstra)

according to special specifications, with the aim to re-create this type of sward. In 1995 the grass was laid over the whole area, including the *plates-bandes* (borders), after which the patterns were cut out. The amount of turf used in 1701/2 shows that it was laid exactly according to the design. There was no surplus turf which required cutting off.

Good maintenance of the 1995 turf is decisive for the general appearance of the garden (fig. 6). The maintenance of the greens at Oxford and Cambridge still follows ancient practice. Gardening equipment has changed, however, and although the scythe was the cutting tool in general use until the beginning of this century, it has been superseded gradually by the rotary mower since the mid-nineteenth century. Reintroduction of the scythe at Hampton Court is not being considered, because it is believed that virtually the same result is obtained with a well-adjusted multiblade rotary mower. Nevertheless, care should be taken that some of the shortcomings of rotary mowers will not show, such as scalping of uneven areas and edges, and ribbing of the grass. The latter problem may be prevented by using a rotary mower with a higher number of blades, the former requires a skilled operator. The tricky areas around the cut-work of the grass need special attention, and it may be necessary to finish these difficult parts off with hedge-shears.

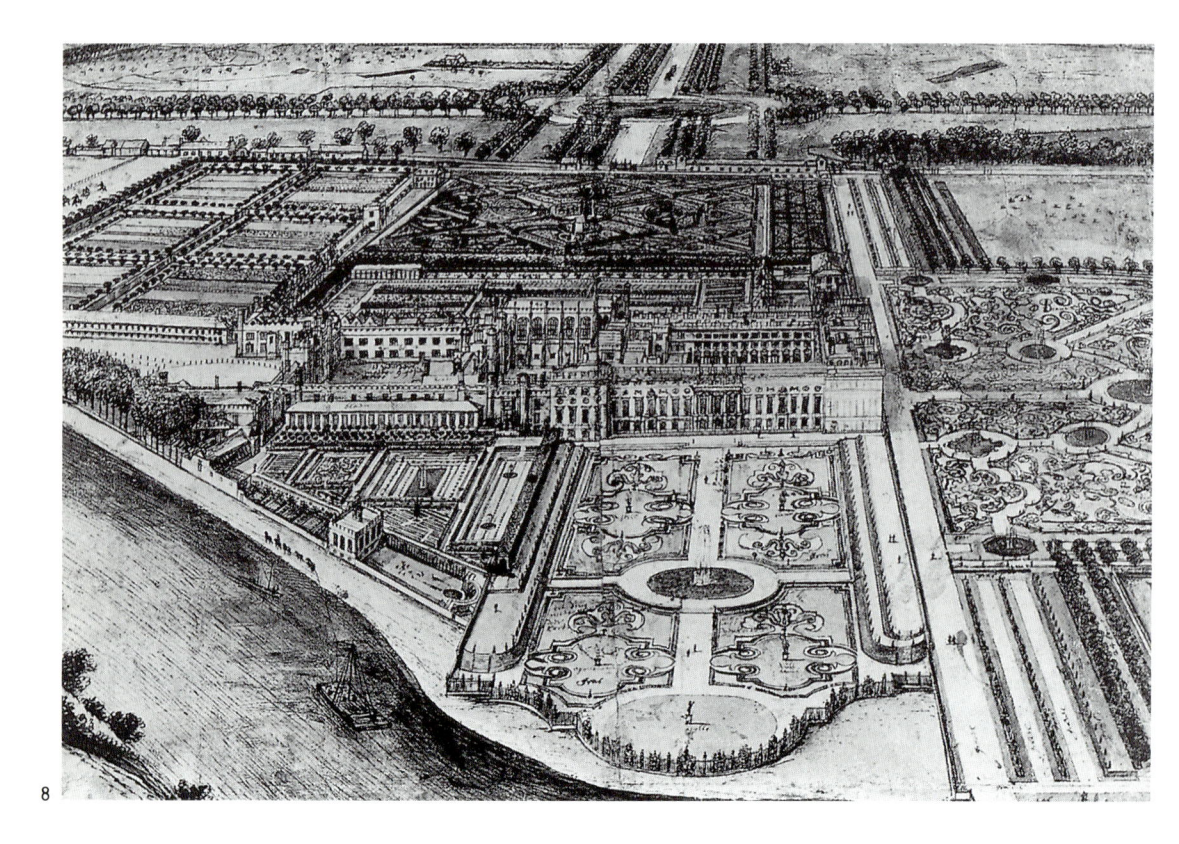

8

Rolling is important to get an even surface in the initial period, but in the long run it compacts the soil, inhibiting plant growth. Some light rolling is, however, considered to be beneficial. A roller attached to the rotary mower will be helpful, but may be insufficient in itself. The striping effect which may be caused by rotary lawnmowers is by some seen as undesirable and unhistorical. However, it is not caused by the mower but by the roller attached to it.[1] Since this effect is produced by the roller only, contemporary equipment could also have caused it, technically speaking; so it cannot be said to be historically incorrect from an aesthetic point of view. However, no historical references to stripy lawns have been found, and current opinion clearly associates stripes with lawnmowers. Therefore, the advice is that stripes should be avoided, until more facts will come to light.

DUTCH BOX EDGING Garden archaeology has not yet produced any facts about the edging of the various compartments in the garden. The word edging has historically been used for anything forming a barrier between two materials, a border or fringe – boards, stone, bricks, tiles, bones, box, grass and several plant species. The purpose of edging was to stop the different materials such as gravel, sand, earth, etc. from mixing after rainfall or maintenance work.

9

8 Leonard Knyff. *Sketch Depicting Hampton Court from the South.* c.1702. Pen and ink. The Trustees of the British Museum

9 Leonard Knyff. *Hampton Court from the East.* c.1702. Oil on canvas. The Royal Collection, Her Majesty The Queen

Although all these materials would have been suitable for flower-gardens with straight beds, they were less so for the curvilinear shapes of the Privy Garden, and plants would have been more suitable for the purpose. Dwarf box was particularly recommended as an edging. Towards the end of the Middle Ages, the Dutch seem to have chosen the dwarf strain of box (*Buxus sempervirens* L. 'Suffruticosa') especially for the purpose of edging. Elsewhere, it is mentioned after 1500.

Box was imported from the Netherlands to Hampton Court in 1691, probably for the construction of the Fountain Garden, and it remained known as Dutch box in the early eighteenth century. Contemporary sources show that well-maintained box edging was trimmed to a maximum width and height of four inches. Larger edging of about a foot was rejected and considered to be 'rude hedges'. Box edging for delineating broderie-work used to be kept at a similar height (under four inches), since larger dimensions would have made it impossible to appreciate the tracery. The recorded quantity of box edging, a total of 762 yards, hardly tallies with the total of 2,420 yards required. It can only be assumed that this was an omission in the accounts (see pp.116-117).

2 Planting design of the Privy Garden[2]

THE PARTERRES   In the planting of the *plates-bandes*, according to the plant lists in the Accounts of the Privy Garden, three different elements can be identified: the shaped trees, comprising pyramids and round-headed trees; tall and low evergreen and deciduous shrubs; and bulbous plants (figs.1, 2, 3 and 8). Unfortunately, the lists were incomplete and not all plant material was noted; some of it may have been reused from the previous layout of the garden, or it may have been paid out of other funds. One list appears to have concerned only the area of the lower garden, which made it possible to analyse the planting in greater detail (see p.118).

Determining the original positions of the yews and hollies was a relatively straightforward process. Information obtained from the ring dating, together with an archaeological reconstruction of the *plates-bandes*, proved that only a few of the trees were in the exact positions of 1701. However, most positions appeared to be in alignment along an east-west axis, including the few historical tree positions, and it was therefore assumed that although the original trees had disappeared, their approximate positions had been preserved in later replants. At the same time, it was found that some minor alterations had been introduced since the initial layout, which might have required slight modifications in tree positions. The removal of the central *plates-bandes* had coincided with an extension of the *plates-bandes* surrounding each of the quarters. A large gap between the last holly trees at the central *plates-bandes* would have been too conspicuous; it was apparently adjusted by reducing the gaps between these trees, and possibly by adjusting the spacing of the next pairs of trees. It seems that, in principle, the trees were planted with a 16-foot spacing, slight differences being spread over two or more spacings, and that they were in alignment along an east-west axis. This corresponds to the eight-foot module used for the garden, as determined by the archaeologists.

Having the distribution of trees fit in with the number of trees mentioned in the accounts was another matter. Yew pyramids of different quality and sizes were supplied; there were both round-headed and pyramid hollies; pyramid true phillyreas and round-headed alaternus. There may also have been an unknown number of trees reused from the previous layout. When we compare the pyramid-shaped and round-headed trees with the trees depicted in the Knyff painting (fig. 9), it proves to be impossible to make the numbers tally without altering the design concept (see drawings T1 and T2, here figs. 10a and 10b). Moreover, Knyff was not consistent in his painting and his drawing, and shows orange trees in the corner positions in one illustration and pyramids in the other. Similarly, the Soane Museum plan (fig. 3) is not very helpful either, as the numbers do not agree, although the basic pattern of yew-holly-yew seems to agree with that of the – round-headed tree – pyramid of the recent survey (see drawings T3 and T4, figs. 10c and 10d). From this it may be concluded that the basic disposition of the latter layout has survived. Besides, the Soane Museum plan showed six pyramids around the Tijou circle, and their existence was confirmed by archaeology.

In the end it proved possible, by using the accounts, to produce a convincing layout which tied the different strands of topographical evidence together. The first bill, which concerns the area of the lower garden, appears to correspond to the other evidence, but lacks any reference to pyramids intended for the middle of the central *plates-bandes*. There would have been a few obvious gaps in the northern area, which would have been filled in for reasons of symmetry at the second phase. These include two of the cheap large yew trees which might have been positioned at the corners during the winter, to be replaced with orange trees in tubs during the summer (fig. 13). The practice of placing orange trees at the corners of the layout was common in other London and Wise gardens, where separate squares were frequently provided for this purpose. The plant numbers for the Privy Garden appear to suggest a seasonal change. This is confirmed by the Knyff drawing (fig. 1), which shows pyramids at the corners, whereas the painting clearly shows trees in tubs. The special trees, pyramid hollies, pyramid true phillyreas, round-headed alaternus and shaped trees, were given central positions, where they made more impact.

Most of the shaped trees were provided with timber sticks or iron rods with gilded knobs for support. The total number of yews and hollies in the parterres is 160, and the accounts show that there were 104 green sticks and 40 ditto rods with golden knobs; that is, a total of 144 supports. If the sixteen pyramid hollies in the centre of the parterres had no sticks, it means that every other yew and holly had been supplied with a support. The 40 iron rods most likely went to the

L104/T1

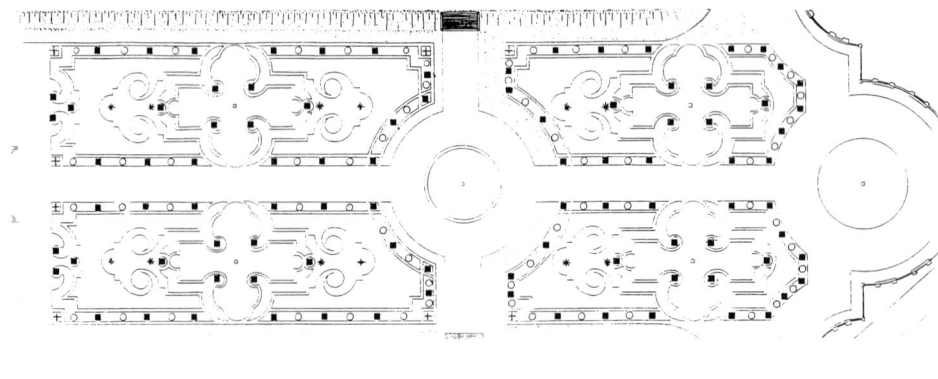

KEY
- ○ 62 round headed
- ■ 94 pyramids
- + 8 tubs in plates-bandes
- ✱ 12 tubs in parterre area

L104/T2

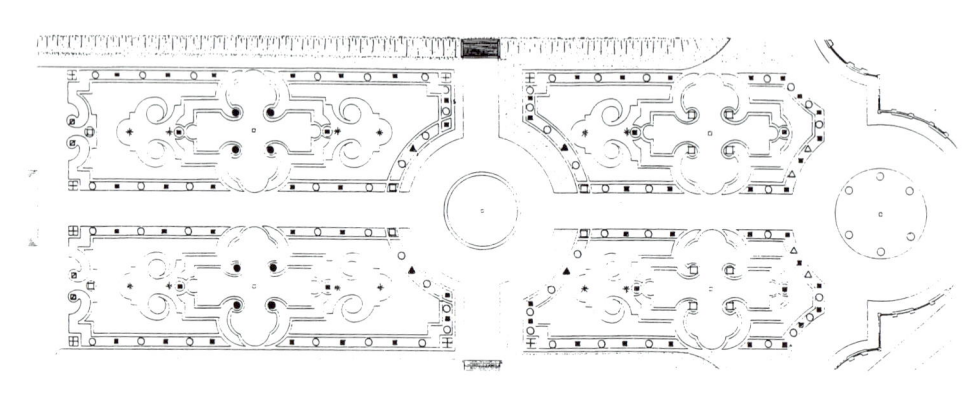

KEY
- ○ 64 large round headed hollies
- ● 8 pyramid hollies
- ■ 54 large pyramid yews
- ☐ 14 large yews
- ▨ 4 shaped yews
- △ 4 round headed alaternus
- ▲ 4 pyramid phillyreas
- + 8 orange trees in tubs (not on plant lists)
- ✱ 12 orange trees in tubs (not on plant lists)

L104/T3

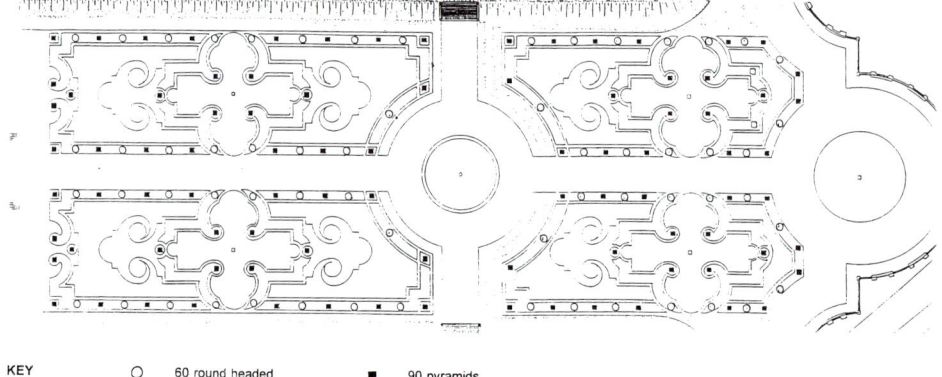

KEY
- ○ 60 round headed
- ■ 90 pyramids
- ☐ 2 pyramids omitted from total count (suspected draughting error)

J.Woudstra *The design of the Privy Garden at Hampton Court*

L104/T4

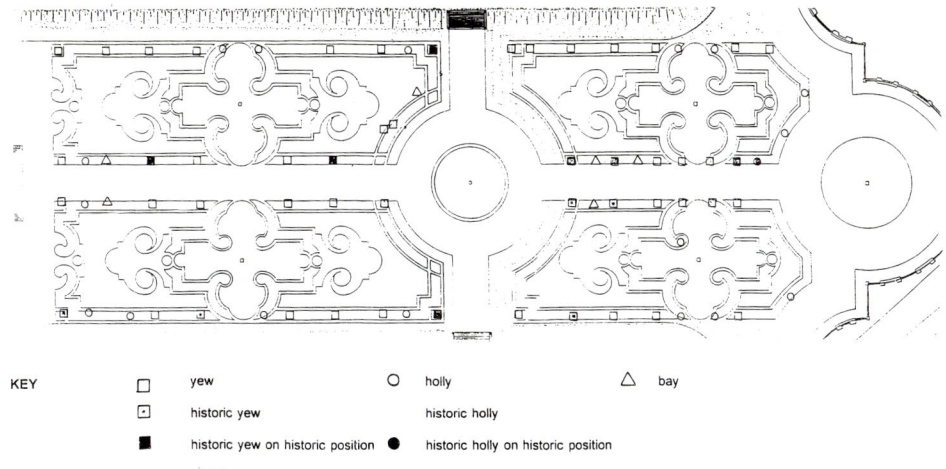

KEY

☐ yew   ◯ holly   △ bay
⊡ historic yew   ⊙ historic holly
■ historic yew on historic position   ● historic holly on historic position

NOTE Historic tree is defined as a tree dating back to the early 1700s or before
Historic position is defined as a tree on a plausible contemporary position as estimated from the archaeologists' reconstruction of the parterre

L104/T5

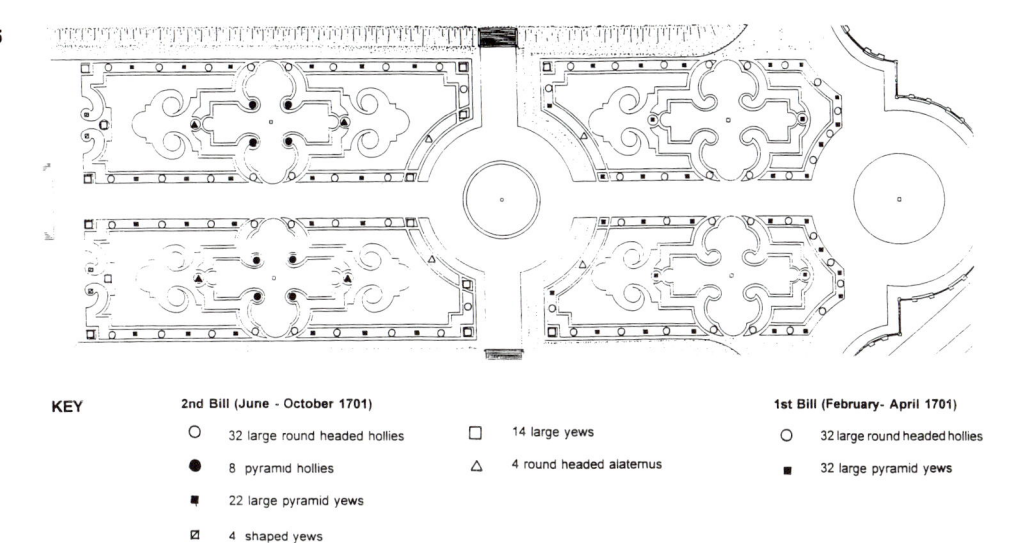

KEY

2nd Bill (June - October 1701)

◯ 32 large round headed hollies
● 8 pyramid hollies
■ 22 large pyramid yews
⊠ 4 shaped yews
▲ 4 pyramid true phillyreas

☐ 14 large yews
△ 4 round headed alaternus

1st Bill (February- April 1701)

◯ 32 large round headed hollies
■ 32 large pyramid yews

10 Laurence Pattacini. Hampton Court Palace, Reconstruction of the Privy Garden, Drawings T1-T5, Oct. 1994

10a Drawing T1: Shaped tree positions in the parterre as indicated on the Leonard Knyff painting (see fig. 9)

10b Drawing T2: Idem, but in relationship with PRO WORK 5/52

10c Drawing T3: Shaped tree positions in the parterre as indicated on the Soane Museum plan (see fig. 3)

10d Drawing T4: Recent survey of shaped tree positions based on 1983 Travers Morgan Survey and 1991 Plowman Craven Survey with additional Archaeologist's information

10e Drawing T5: Reconstruction of shaped tree positions in the parterres based on plant list in 1701 PRO WORK

38 yews in the upper parterre and the two shaped yews in the corner positions of the lower parterres, which were replaced with orange trees in tubs during the summer (see drawing T5, fig. 10e).[3] Iron rods were only rarely used in English gardens, although they have been described at Dyrham.[4] These rods did, however, appear in contemporary Dutch engravings, such as the garden of Mr. Van Haveren, near Amsterdam.[5]

The location of the shrubs in *plates-bandes* was related to that of the shaped trees. The shrubs listed might be grouped as large standards, according to size and habit – 76 roses (*Rosa sp.*), 76 sweet briars (*Rosa rubiginosa* L.) and 38 syringas (*Philadelphus coronarius* L.); medium-sized standards, 161 honeysuckles (*Lonicera sp.*); and small shrubs, 62 savins (*Juniperus sabina* L.), 50 lavender (*Lavandula angustifolia* L.), 56 striped rhus (*Coriaria myrtifolia* L. 'Variegata'). The total number of large shrubs divided by the total number of spaces available between the shaped trees in the *plates-bandes* gives a basic pattern or rhythm of two large shrubs between each pair of shaped trees, with a low shrub between each pair of larger plants (fig. 11). This pattern could be varied slightly at the semicircular outer *plates-bandes* and substantially in the central *plates-bandes*, since there would have been a deficiency of larger shrubs at this point. Here, two honeysuckles could have been interspersed between each pair of larger shrubs, requiring twenty plants in each of the quarters of the emblem – a total of 160 plants. The historical number was 161, remarkably enough an odd number, which cannot be explained in a supposedly symmetrical scheme.

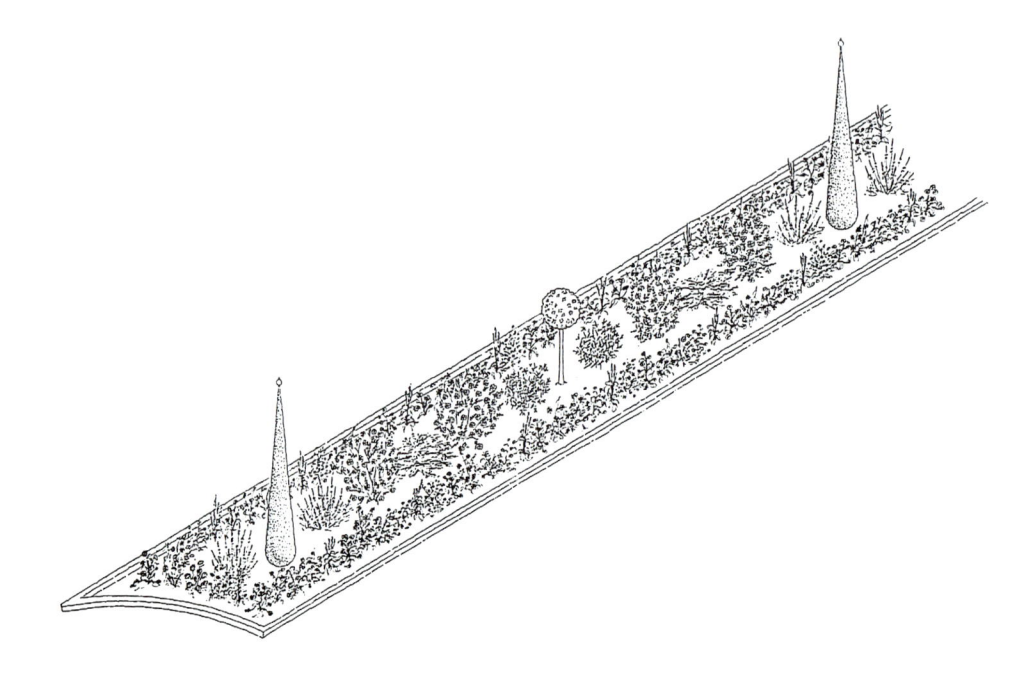

The distribution of the other species must have been determined by the numbers of plants available, with probably two different types of roses between each pair of topiary trees, and a syringa at each corner and replacing shaped trees where they ought to have been if the rhythm had been maintained regardless of the design. This layout would have left the right number of pairs of roses to be interspersed with savin, while yew pyramids would have been flanked by lavender, and the hollies by striped rhus on either side. Such an arrangement of short shrubby plants underneath the hollies might explain the engravings of the 1730s of the Fountain Garden, where the hollies were depicted standing over square-clipped plants. It was not possible, in the end, to establish the exact

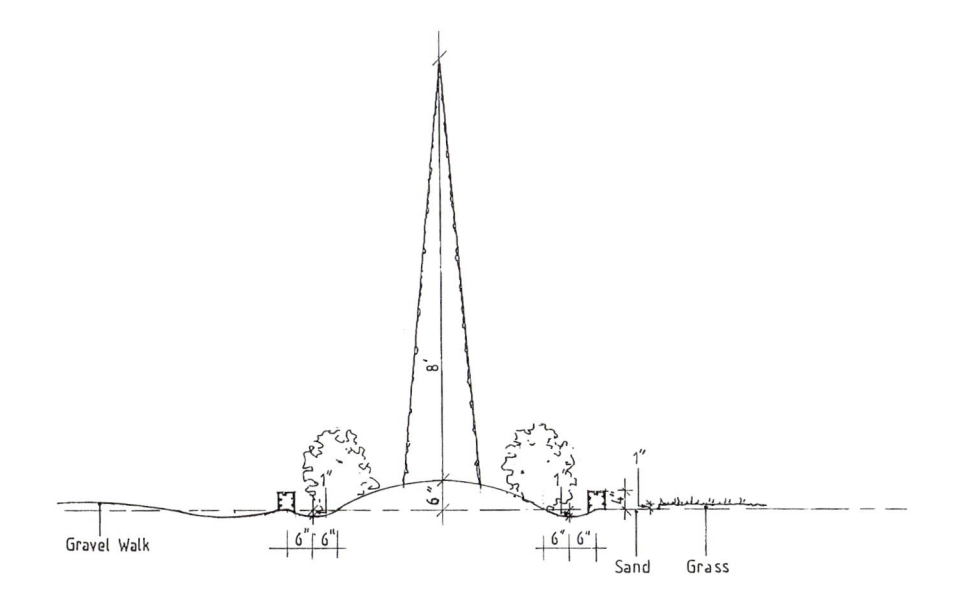

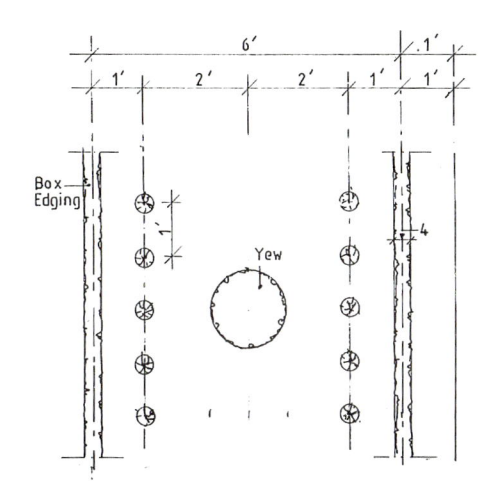

11 Laurence Pattacini. Reconstruction of the spacing of shaped trees, drawing done in 1994.

12 Laurence Pattacini. Reconstruction of the arrangement of the gravel walk, *plate-bande*, sand and grass, showing planting positions, drawing done in 1994.

number of plants which were used in the scheme suggested above; two extra roses were required and one honeysuckle was left over.

The distribution of the bulb and herbaceous planting in the 1701 garden at Hampton Court is largely a matter of conjecture. From the fairly small number of bulbs ordered for the Privy Garden, it has already been established that a French system of multiple rows with a four-inch spacing along the edge of the *plates-bandes* could not have been maintained.[6] This may not be surprising, considering that the gardener in charge, Mr. Quellenberg, was a Dutchman. The method of planting was not very Dutch either, due to the high content of woody plants, which was more consistent with the fairly dense planting of shrubs found in English borders (figs.14 and 15). The intended effect would probably have been more like that depicted in the Thacker painting of Longleat, which also agrees with the proposed model for the shrubby element of the planting, rather than what was depicted in the Lambert painting of 10 Downing Street, where plants were individually spaced. Thacker depicted a fairly dense herbaceous planting below the shrubs and shaped trees. How much of this is artistic licence is impossible to say, as the uniformly low size of the herbaceous planting and the very low size of the shrubs make the view slightly dubious with respect to the proportions.

13

The first reliable evidence, the Goodwood planting plan, is of a much later date and hardly admissible as contemporary evidence for Hampton Court. Besides, the 1735 Goodwood border lacks a shrub and shaped-tree content, and given the total number of crocus used in the Privy Garden, it could not have been planted like Goodwood – a continuous line with a two-inch spacing. While further research will be carried out regarding this aspect of the planting, with some element of experimenting, the character of the central row served as a guideline for other planting. The extent of the central row dictated that there could be only one additional row of plants on either side. These rows will ultimately contain small groups of bulbs, annuals and perennials, with two basic changes in the course of the year – as seems to have been common practice – for spring and for summer display.[7]

THE TERRACES   The terraces were probably planted after the trees in the parterres had been positioned. The terraces contained only yew pyramids, and the accounts indicate the supply and planting of 76 specimens. Unlike the area of the parterre, which was still planted in 1991, the terraces revealed much more archaeological information, since they had been cleared at some stage and were maintained as grass banks. The information revealed a complicated

13 Evidence showed that orange trees in a tub were positioned at the garden's corners during the summer, to be replaced with pyramid yews in autumn (summer 1995). (Photo: Jan Woudstra)

14 Development of the summer planting during the first year (summer 1995). (Photo: Jan Woudstra)

sequence of tree planting on the western terrace, while on the eastern terrace it appeared to be simpler, although many of the historical tree pits were large and had been extended. However, when the two terraces were compared, it was possible to reconstruct the scenario of how it came about.

The planting probably started on the western terrace. Pits were dug with a 16-foot spacing, starting at the south end, possibly from the top of the southern steps down. The 16-foot grid continued irrespective of the central steps along the terraces, and a total of twenty-three positions can be identified. The archaeologists did not find any evidence of tree positions belonging to this grid near the northern steps. At this point, it seems that the tree positions did not line up with the opening in the centre of the bower, nor with the statues in the centre of the parterres. A new grid was then dug to give a 16-foot gap in front of the opening to the bower.

The new grid was set out simultaneously on the west and east terraces. On the east there was no evidence of an abandoned grid; on the western terrace, evidence has helped to confirm the new tree positions. The new grid started from the central steps to the north and to the south, once again with a basic 16-foot grid, with adjustments. At first it seems that the trees in the northern part of the terraces were made to line up with the trees in the *plates-bandes*. This could be done simply by enlarging some of the holes of the previous 16-foot grid. This connection with the trees in the *plates-bandes* was lost to the north of the central opening in the bower, nor could it be maintained at the southern end. Similar to what happened in the *plates-bandes*, it appears that the surplus space to the south side was divided into equal parts, which resulted in two 14-foot spacings, the most southerly pyramids lining up with the trees in the *plates-bandes*.

On the east side, the tree positions mirrored those on the west terrace, except for a section in the centre, where the spacing was adjusted to allow for a 16-foot gap opposite the statue in the centre of the parterre. The 16-foot grid continues to the north end. A total of 45 trees were required for the west terrace, and 52 trees for the east terrace; that is, a grand total of 97 trees. This amount could not be verified, as the accounts mentioned only 76; it is possible that the rest was supplied from elsewhere in the garden.

THE QUEEN'S BOWER   The Queen's Bower was situated on the west terrace in the garden where it had been erected in 1689, and consisted of a wooden framework planted with wych-elm. Although the framework had decayed sometime in the eighteenth century, the wych-elms survived until they fell prey to Dutch elm disease in the mid-1970s. The ancient elms were then replaced with a metal framework covered by hornbeam. At an early stage of the restoration programme, the expensive option of reconstructing the bower was discussed, in relation to refurbishing and adapting the existing one. The latter option did not really fit in with the restoration philosophy of the Agency, which was to restore the garden as much as possible to its early-eighteenth-century condition. Horticulturists also suggested that it would be difficult to adapt the existing hornbeams from the existing low squared top to a higher arched shape. It was therefore decided that the existing bower would have to be replaced (fig. 16).

Archaeological investigation, as part of the work on the central steps up the terraces, revealed that there was very little useful evidence left; actually, the archaeologists decided that from the way the 1970s bower had been removed it seemed unlikely that anything would be found. One thing the investigation did reveal was evidence of a sill beam resting on top of triangular buttresses. These brick buttresses, built to a nine-foot module, formed a retaining structure for the western boundary wall of the garden. The top layer of bricks had been roughly hewn out over a width of about one foot, forming what was thought to be a groove for the sill beam on which the bower rested at either side. Other findings revealed a section where the buttresses had been broken up, for which the archaeologists were unable to provide an explanation.

Since no evidence could be discovered of how wide these arches, and thus the bower, had been, it was necessary to resort to research into other possibilities. Contemporary sources revealed evidence concerning the construction of bowers. Here, John Evelyn's unpublished manuscript for a book entitled *Elysium Britannicum* was particularly illuminating. Evelyn had described the predecessor of the Queen's Bower at Hampton Court (also probably in the Privy Garden) in his diary as '... The cradle-work of hornbeam in the garden is for the perplexed twining of the trees very observable'. In his *Elysium Britannicum*, he suggested how bowers might be constructed, considering 12 feet a graceful height and building it of six-inch square cleft oak uprights and rails of four by two inches. He noted that hornbeam was most suitable for the purpose of covering these structures, but that elm and field maple might be selected instead. He initially recommended a planting distance of a yard, but this was later altered to one foot.

Several other authors referred to bowers and their construction, while information on some actually built examples has been very precise and reconstructions could, and have been, undertaken from them. One such instance is the Queen's Bower at Het Loo, where William III had been advised on its construction by Hans Willem Bentinck, whose bower at Zorgvliet was very similar – also, remarkably, to one of Daniel Marot's published designs. Dr. Harris, in his *Description of the King's Royal Palace and Gardens at Loo* of 1699, has described in detail how the bower had been constructed, giving dimensions for the width and openings, while another visitor noted that it had been built of oak. With the benefit of contemporary illustrations and extremely limited archaeological research, the reconstruction of the bower at Het Loo was a relatively simple exercise. On inspection of the bower at Het Loo, one can see that concessions had to be made to comply with engineering and health and safety requirements. There are iron stretching bars at ten-foot intervals, the arches themselves consist of laminated wood (a modern invention), as opposed to mortise-and-tenon sections, and the bower has been built of a durable tropical hardwood, as opposed to oak.

Although there was no such detailed information for the Queen's Bower at Hampton Court, there was the advantage that the wych-elms which originally covered the wooden structure had survived until modern times. It was thought that information on the spacing between the trees, their height and the width of the surviving trees would determine the dimensions of the original bower. However, there was no reliable information on these trees from before the time they were removed, and the most recent photographs dated from the first years of this century. Although it was possible, with the aid of the photographs, to determine the width and height of the original bower at 10 and $16\frac{1}{2}$ feet respectively, there still appeared to be a relatively large margin of error, estimated at about ten per cent, depending on which method was being used. As no further information seemed likely, sketch designs were produced on this basis, and on that of the limited information from the 1689 WORK accounts. This showed that the structure had been built with oak and fir rails and was later painted in a green colour.

15

A breakthrough came when further limited archaeological research was commissioned at the north end near the steps, in order to detect whether there might be any additional surviving evidence. This excavation proved to be a great success; accurate information was produced on the original construction and dimensions by the discovery of the slots for the first uprights of the bower, and the sill beams. The timbers used in the original construction could now be accurately determined at five inches, the width of the bower at 12 (not 10) feet and the height at 18 (not 16½) feet. Thus, this evidence resulted in a much larger and more dominating structure than had previously been assumed.

Still to be answered were the questions about the length of the bower, the spacing of the individual arches and the position of the opening(s) in the bower's centre. This opening had been based on the 1689 layout of the garden, but was retained when the gardens were altered in the early eighteenth century. After the archaeologists had investigated the positions of the yew pyramids, and their findings had been analysed, it became clear that the original opening might be determined by this new information. Instead of a discrepancy in the spacing of the pyramids in the centre of the garden to allow for a vista to the

15 Development of the summer planting during the first year (summer 1995). (Photo: Jan Woudstra)

16 The bower was rebuilt following old methods, but some modifications were necessary to comply with modern health and safety regulations (winter 1994/95). (Photo: Jan Woudstra)

Materials used for the changes to the Privy Garden in 1701/2 (PRO WORK 5/52)

Item	folio	quantity
Gravel for walks	571	508 solid yards 6" thick fine gravel
	581	1007 solid yards fine screened gravel
	451	214 solid yards fine gravel round circle
Sand for alleys	571	625 superficiall yards
	581	2417 superficiall yards
Black earth for borders	570	422 solid yards
	570	1702 solid yards (wrought three times)
	580	951 solid yards (mixt with rotten dung... wrought and mixt 3 times)
Earth underneath turf	581	698 solid yards earth
	581	1134 solid yards loamy earth for turf slopes
	451	137 solid yards [for circle and screen?]
Turf	571	4412 superficiall yards (2 quarters, verges, etc.)
	581	5243 superficiall yards (terraces and verges)
	451	798 superficiall yards (circle and next to stone steps)
Dutch box edging	571	333 running yards
	571	429 running yards

$1" = 1$ inch $= \frac{1}{12}$ foot   1 yard = 3 feet   1 solid yard = 1 cubic yard
1 foot = 0.3048 metre   1 superficiall yard = 1 square yard   1 running yard = 1 yard length

statues in the centre as on the east terrace, the information on the west terrace showed that the opening was slightly further north, and it was assumed that this must have related to the opening in the bower.

The accurate positioning of the opening also helped to determine the spacing of the bower arches. It was assumed from the historical illustrations that the bower opening must have been two sections wide; that is, it must have been either six or eight feet wide, with a height just below the springing-point of 12 feet. The exact distance between the centre point of the bower and the north end was 148 feet, which corresponded with a four-foot spacing of the individual arches. From the Knyff and Kip engraving of the west side, it appears that there was also an opening on the wall-side of the bower, which might have served as a niche for a garden seat with a view across the garden.

The final question concerned the original length of the bower and its length

Measurements of the 1701/2 layout compared with those of the 1995 reconstruction of the Privy Garden

Items	1701/2	1995 (measured)	1701/2 calculated thickness
GRAVEL			
Apollo circle	214 cu yrds	1660 sq yrds	$4\frac{3}{5}$" (area difficult to define; 6" allows for only 1284 sq yrds)
Other walks	1515 cu yrds	5503 sq yrds	$9\frac{9}{10}$"
total	1729 cu yrds	7163 sq yrds	$8\frac{3}{5}$" average
SAND			
total	3042 sq yrds	1090 sq yrds	difference 1952 sq yrds; thickness not known (in other areas archival evidence indicates 6" thickness for sand alleys)
BLACK EARTH FOR BORDERS			
total	3075 cu yrds	(archaeological evidence suggests an average depth of about 3 ft)	l x w x h = 3075 cu yrds 3085' x 6' x h = 3075 2057 x h = 3075 h = c. 5 ft
EARTH UNDERNEATH TURF			
Terraces	1134 cu yrds	4611 sq yrds	1134 : 5243 x 36 = $7\frac{8}{10}$"
Apollo circle	137 cu yrds	814 sq yrds	137 : 798 x 36 = $6\frac{2}{10}$"
Parterres	698 cu yrds	5027 sq yrds	698 : 4412 x 36" = $5\frac{7}{10}$"
TURF			
Terraces	5243 sq yrds	4611 sq yrds	not applicable
Apollo circle & Tijou screen	798 sq yrds	814 sq yrds	
Parterres & along walks	4412 sq yrds	5027 sq yrds	
total	10,453 sq yrds	10,452 sq yrds	difference 1 sq yrd
DUTCH BOX EDGING			
total	762 yrds	2420 yrds	difference 1658 yrds

in the early eighteenth century. Investigation did not extend far enough south to be conclusive about this, and other aspects had to be researched.

From the WORK accounts it was known that the bower had a front attached to it, which was shown in several Knyff illustrations on the northern end as a classical portico, crowned by three balls. The Knyff drawing, however (fig. 1), also showed a portico at the southern end of the bower, of a different design

Plant Bills relating to the making of the Privy Garden (1701)

			£ : s : d	£ : s : d
FIRST BILL (FEBRUARY TO APRIL 1701): PRO WORK 5/52, f. 572				
76	Standard Roses	at 6d Per tree	1 : 18 : 00	
76	Standard Sweet Bryers	at 6d	1 : 18 : 00	
161	Standard honeySuckles in Basketts	at 2s 0d	16 : 02 : 00	
38	Standard Syringoes	at 2s 0d	3 : 16 : 00	
32	Large Round headed holleys	at 50s Per tree (40s)	64 : 00 : 00	
32	Large Pyramid Yews	at 20s Per tree	32 : 00 : 00	
62	Savins	at 4s Per tree	12 : 08 : 00	
56	Lavenders	at 6d Per plant	1 : 08 : 00	
56	Stript Rhus	at 6d Per plant	01 : 08 : 00	
SECOND BILL (JUNE TO OCTOBER 1701): PRO WORK 5/52, f. 581				Price as paid
32	Large round headed Holleys	at 50s each (45s)	80 : 00 : 00	72 : 00 : 00
8	Pyramid Holleys	at 2£ each (36s)	16 : 00 : 00	14 : 08 : 00
4	Pyramid True Phillareas	at 50s each	10 : 00 : 00	10 : 00 : 00
22	Large Pyramid Yews	at 3£ each (55s)	66 : 00 : 00	60 : 00 : 00
4	Shaped Yews	at 25s each	5 : 00 : 00	5 : 10 : 00
4	Round headed allaternus	at 6s each	1 : 04 : 00	1 : 04 : 00
76	yews for ye sloopes	at 5s each	19 : 00 : 00	19 : 00 : 00
14	Large Yews	at 10s each	7 : 00 : 00	7 : 00 : 00
2000	Tulips	at 8s Per Cent	8 : 00 : 00	8 : 00 : 00
2000	White Narcissus	at 4s Per Cent	4 : 00 : 00	4 : 00 : 00
2000	Crocuses	at 2s Per Cent	2 : 00 : 00	2 : 00 : 00
800	Hyacinths	at 10s Per Cent	4 : 00 : 00	4 : 00 : 00
500	Bulbous Iris	at 5s Per Cent	1 : 05 : 00	1 : 05 : 00

Note: Last columns denote cost of plant material in pounds (£) : shillings (s) and pence (d)

with a rounded top without balls. The latter was not shown in any other illustrations. The archaeologists had decided that there was no evidence for this structure, as the southern end of the bower had not survived beyond 96 yards from the northern steps. The original bower clearly reached south of this point, and different theories emerged on what had happened to it. An opening in the wall at 104 yards from the northern steps might have defined the maximum extent; probably, the original end was situated between 96 and 104 yards. The new stone steps up the centre of the terraces in the early-eighteenth-century layout would have met the southern end of the bower, and in order to improve this relationship the last arch or few arches of the bower would have been demolished. This scenario helped to explain why the southern end of the bower was not shown in later illustrations. The end of the bower as reconstructed was therefore defined by the position of the steps.

One other aspect subject to an even greater degree of conjecture was the reconstruction of the northern end (or portico) of the bower. While a surviving drawing of it was originally thought to be included in the so-called Fort drawings, this did not quite tally with the bower dimensions, and as no other information came to light, this design was adapted and reinterpreted. Since the southern bower appears to have been demolished as part of the laying-out of the early-eighteenth-century garden, it will not be reconstructed. The bower itself has been reconstructed to a height of 18 and a width of 12 feet, with a total of 73 arches spaced at four-foot centres. There are two openings in the bower, one on the garden and one on the wall-side, opposite each other. Like in 1689, the bower was built with oak uprights and ribs, and fir rails. As at Het Loo, some concessions had to be made for health and safety reasons, because a modern engineering report showed that the historical structure 'could not have stood up'. This is why, instead of wooden dowels, stainless steel bolts were used to tie the uprights to the ribs. This will not be visible, however, since the bolts were sunk and covered with wooden plugs. Again as at Het Loo, metal rods had to be inserted for structural stability. It will not be possible to start painting the bower for a number of years, because paint does not adhere to green oak. Research with respect to the right colour has already produced samples of historically correct verdigris paint, which will be tested for durability while the oak of the bower weathers.

The bower was not planted with wych-elm because Dutch elm disease is still prevalent; instead, as mentioned above, hornbeam was used. The approximate spacing shown in an early-twentieth-century survey of the palace indicates that the (slightly irregular) original spacing may have been about four feet, suggesting that some thinning must have taken place. The same four-foot spacing was used for the 1970s hornbeams; it was said that the trees were replanted at the positions of the original elms, but this could not be confirmed. Therefore, the suggested original spacing was four or two feet. Since an immediate effect was required with regard to the planting, it was decided to choose a two-foot spacing.

3 Conclusion

Although archival records may be verified with the aid of archaeology, soil analysis and surviving plants, it is obvious that there will always remain some areas which are open to doubt. Contemporary evidence is needed to fill in the gaps, but it has to be reviewed regularly and modified when more information becomes available. The reconstruction of the bower, for example, not only illustrates the significance of the archaeological findings, but also shows that no full reconstruction is possible without proper archival knowledge, in combination with sufficient information on contemporary practice. The next stage is the maintenance of the garden, and this paper has hinted at its importance for the way a garden should look and 'feel'. Maintenance is also something to be reckoned with before undertaking a garden's reconstruction.

PRO WORK   Kew, Public Record Office, WORK accounts

1 See S. M. Goulty, *Heritage Gardens: Care, Conservation and Management*, London / New York, 1993, p. 88.
2 This section on 'Planting Design of the Privy Garden' was previously published in Simon Thurley et al., *The King's Privy Garden at Hampton Court Palace 1689-1995*, London, 1995.
3 PRO WORK, 5/51, f. 360, f. 450.
4 S. Switzer, *Ichnographia Rustica*, 1718, p. 118, describes them as 'large pyramid silver hollies, ews, &c. having painted iron rods with gilded nobs for their support...'
5 M. Brouërius van Niedeck, *Het verheerlykt Watergraefs- of Diemer-meer By de Stadt Amsterdam, Vertoont in verscheide vermakelyke Gezichten*, Amsterdam, 1725, plate 20.
6 However, the French practice may have been adopted at Hampton Court in the 1730s, judging from the Tinney engravings of the Fountain Garden.
7 The Goodwood planting plan was transcribed and published by M. Laird and J. Harvey in *Garden History*, 21 (1993), 2, pp. 158-205.

Batey, Mavis, and Jan Woudstra. *The Story of the Privy Garden at Hampton Court*. London: Barn Elms, 1995.
Environmental Design Associates. 'Maintenance Plan; the Privy Garden, Hampton Court Palace'. Draft. May 1995.
Thurley, Simon; David Jacques; Jan Woudstra; and Brian Dix. *The King's Privy Garden at Hampton Court Palace*. London: Apollo, 1995.
Woudstra, Jan. 'De reconstructie van de Privy Garden, Hampton Court Palace'. *Groen*, 52 (1996), 4, pp. 32-38.

Terraced gardens in Central Europe from the fifteenth to the eighteenth century: Problems of conservation

GÉZA HAJÓS

HISTORICAL BACKGROUND: IN HUNGARY   Terraced gardens make their first appearance in Central Europe at the end of the fifteenth century, when the humanist Hungarian king Matthias Corvinus commissioned Chimenti Camicia some time after 1480 to create so-called 'hanging gardens' (*giardino pensile*) for his Buda castle (fig. 2).[1] The huge *cisterna regia* for these gardens has been preserved, together with its ice-house. Camicia was a collaborator of Francesco di Giorgio, who had become famous in Central Italy and elsewhere for his sophisticated technical innovations in garden design. Vicenzo Scamozzi writes that his father admired a magnificent pump on his visit to Hungary, which supplied river water for the hanging gardens of Buda Castle high above the Danube.[2] In emulation of the Italian spirit, Matthias Corvinus required that the garden should be opened up to the landscape. The peripheral walls of this, unfortunately now vanished, *giardino pensile* were studded with openings, called *oculi*, from which the lovely panorama of the Buda hills could be viewed. As his chronicler Bonfini describes, the Hungarian king also had *pensile in arce hortos* constructed in the Viennese Hofburg during his brief occupation of the latter between 1485 and 1490.[3] However, the most impressive terraced gardens in Hungary were to be seen in the Corvinian summer palace at Visegrád on the Danube, which were in existence by 1480.[4] No doubt the Visegrád gardens influenced the Holy Roman Emperor Maximilian II (from the House of Habsburg) when he decided to build a new pheasantry ('Neue Fasanerie') on the site where Sultan Suleiman had pitched his tent during the unsuccessful siege of Vienna by the Turks in 1529.

IN AUSTRIA   The Viennese pheasantry was extended in 1570 with a massive 'Neugebäude', emblematic both of victory and of the ruler's pretensions to world power (fig. 1). But it also functioned as a symbol of legitimacy in the sense of continuity with the traditions of antiquity. Close to the Danube watermeadows, two narrow terraces were built fronting the 116-metre-long façade, from where one could enjoy both the distant panorama and the view of the flower gardens lying immediately below.

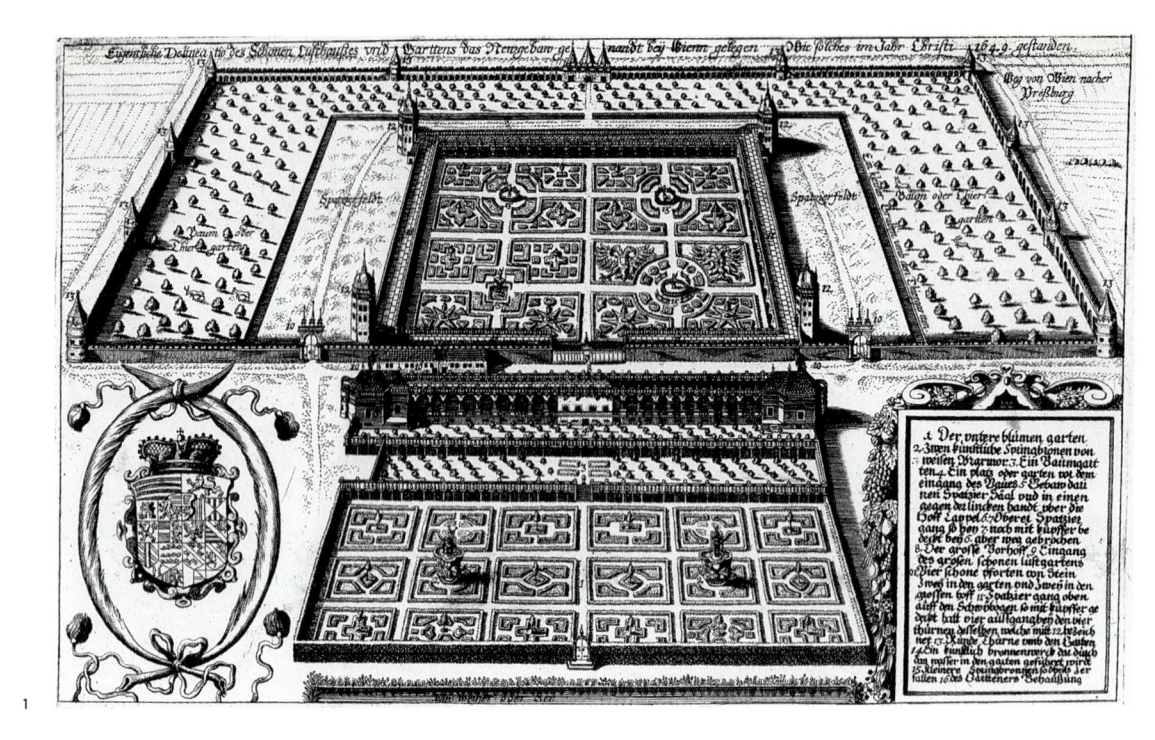

The history of the garden of the Viennese Neugebäude is now well known. I discussed it in some detail at the Clusius Conference in Leiden in 1990 and a description has also been published in *The Authentic Garden*.[5] I will therefore recapitulate only the salient points here. The moving spirit behind the whole complex (apart from the Emperor himself) was the Netherlandish humanist Augier Ghislain de Busbecq, who had been in Turkey between 1553 and 1562 as the imperial ambassador. He brought back from there some interesting ideas, as well as several previously unknown plants such as tulips, together with other ancient curiosities, for which the Neugebäude was to be a sort of museum. Clusius was also active here between 1573 and 1576, heading a substantial team of Walloon gardeners. The architectural concept was in the hands of Jacopo da Strada, who wanted to make the Neugebäude into an enormous 'Antiquarium', similar to the one in Munich. In 1571 the Emperor acquired plans and descriptions of the Villa d'Este at Tivoli from the Cardinal of Ferrara: the plan was to create a similarly impressive 'wonder of the world' in Vienna, a project that unfortunately remained unrealized due to the premature death of its instigator. Emperor Rudolph II moved his seat to Prague and showed little interest in the fulfilment of these ambitious ideas.

Because of the 150-year Turkish occupation of Hungary, few great garden projects were undertaken in the East Austrian area between the late sixteenth and the late seventeenth century. From the beginning of the new prosperity in Austria, a small terraced baroque garden, known as Neuwaldegg, existed in Vienna. The property at Dornbach which incorporated it was acquired in 1691 by Countess Straitmann and a small country house was erected here, which was completed by Baron Bartholotti von Partenfeld, supposedly after designs by the architect Johann Bernhard Fischer von Erlach. From a print made in 1719, we can visualize this garden (fig. 3).[6] In the foreground are richly planted and decorative parterres on six descending terraces. In the garden proper, which is lavishly ornamented with statues, vases, fountains, splendid stairways, luxuriously conceived *parterres de broderie*, topiary trees and hedges, as well as tub plants and climbing frames, ladies and gentlemen of the aristocracy are strolling about. They are entertained by the music of a lute-player as they watch their dogs gambolling here and there.

The artificiality of the Neuwaldegg baroque garden makes it appear as if an angular prismatic structure had been cut into the charming Viennese landscape. It is an architectural setting for terraces (fig. 4), from which, however, even at the beginning of the eighteenth century, the beauties of the surrounding landscape were to be enjoyed with a certain sense of distance. The whole area was thus a self-contained microcosm, a sacred hillside worthy of aristocratic devotion. The surroundings merely acted as a distanced backdrop or wings. In the second half of the eighteenth century, a subsequent owner, the Irish count Moritz Lacy, merged this Hesperidean Isle with the surrounding Wienerwald, transforming it into an 'English garden'.[7] The baroque garden

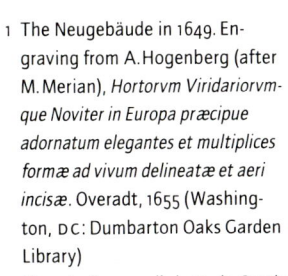

1 The Neugebäude in 1649. Engraving from A. Hogenberg (after M. Merian), *Hortorvm Viridariorvmque Noviter in Europa præcipue adornatum elegantes et multiplices formæ ad vivum delineatæ et aeri incisæ*. Overadt, 1655 (Washington, DC: Dumbarton Oaks Garden Library)

2 The *giardino pensile* in Buda Castle. Illustration from the Hartman-Schedel'sche Chronik, 1493

was simplified about 1770 and played a less important role in the ceremonial aesthetic of this increasingly reclusive nobleman, who nonetheless had made his park accessible to the public.

Another important personality to be interested in the integration of a cosmically ordered garden landscape with the surrounding natural scenery was the prince Eugene of Savoy, who had made a career in the service of the Emperor. His two most magnificent creations – the garden of the Belvedere in Vienna and the Schlosshof garden on the Marchfeld (Lower Austria) – are demonstrations of the two classic types of High Baroque, as defined by the famous French theoretician of architecture Charles d'Aviler.[8]

The Belvedere was built as a gently terraced garden (like Versailles or Marly), while Schlosshof was steeply terraced (like St.-Germain-en-Laye) (figs. 5 and 6, 7 and 8). Both gardens were constructed by the same team, consisting of the architect Johann Lukas von Hildebrandt, the garden designer Dominique Girard (a pupil of Le Nôtre) and the gardener Anton Zinner. All these experts managed to achieve a remarkable degree of creative co-operation. The Belvedere was laid out between 1700 and 1723,[9] while the Schlosshof garden was created between 1729 and 1732.[10]

The name Belvedere first appears in 1750; until then the garden was referred to by a complicated formula: 'the magnificent arena of the wars and victories of the unforgettable hero of our times, Eugenii Francisci, Duke of Savoy and Piedmont'. This nomenclature gave expression to the idea that the entire

3

garden with its Upper and Lower Palaces (and not, as we now say, 'buildings with laid-out gardens', which subordinates the latter to the former) represented the earthly and heavenly apotheosis of the Prince. The art historian Hans Aurenhammer suggests that the view from the Upper Belvedere towards the Kahlenberg (a little mount near Vienna) was not only conceived as an aesthetic experience of landscape, but was also a celebration and memorial of youthful heroism,[11] for it was from the Kahlenberg in 1683 that the young Prince Eugene had his first view of the city, arriving with the army commanded by the Polish king Jan Sobieski to free Vienna from the second Turkish siege. Thus the landscape unfolding from the garden was not so much a landscape of nature as a battle arena, less a place of aesthetic experience than an imagined picture of history.

Although the concept of a 'Belvedere' goes back to the Renaissance, up to the period of the romantic early Enlightenment it was redolent of great estates, political influence and mythopoetic power; but often, also, of chaotic disorder, against which stood the cosmic order of the planned garden.[12] In the Belvedere garden, the visitor followed the war hero 'on his way from the world of the elements and the workings of nature – Pluto and Proserpine, the water gods Neptune and Thetis – up to Parnassus, from which all waters flow, and finally to Olympus, the seat of the Gods';[13] that is to say, from the Lower Belvedere with its bosquets up to the Upper Belvedere with its *parterres de broderie*. Prince Eugene brought together in his Summer Palace many aspects of the natural world (for example in his menagerie and in the orangery), the whole complex thus evoking an 'Island of the Hesperides'. Against this backdrop it was natural that the great statesman and general was often identified with Hercules or Apollo. The sloping site of the Belvedere – at that time outside the city walls – was cleverly chosen and cunningly exploited as a scene for mythological allusion, with terraces, steps and hollows divided into different scenarios for imagined worlds.

A similarly complicated programme was realized on the seven mighty terraces of the Schlosshof gardens. As with the Vienna Belvedere, the view served a political purpose, for it led the eye to the mountains of Hungary (just before 1700 reconquered from the Turks) on the far horizon. Two allegorical figures represent 'the statesmanship of Prince Eugene' and his 'military glory'.[14] The natural features are linked to these, composed of artificial and artistic elements (*parterres de compartiment pour les fleurs*) in the upper region, which descend to the wilder nature below (the wooded areas). Bernardo Bellotto's painstaking views of Schlosshof are an indication for us today of the significance attached to this hunting lodge in the 'glorious Austrian Century'.[15]

3 Neuwaldegg in 1719. Engraving.
(Photo: Géza Hajós)

IN SWITZERLAND   Another terraced garden was laid out in Switzerland at Solothurn for Schloss Waldegg, commissioned by the patrician Johann Viktor von Besenval (1638-1713), who had a glittering international career as intermediary between the Sun-King Louis XIV and the Holy Roman Emperor Leopold I.[16] From 1682 on, he had the longest baroque façade in Switzerland built here, which towards the end of the century received richly decorative additions. The originally semicircular viewing platform of the southern garden was transformed in 1700 into a gateway with steps and a fountain. Thus the entire complex, which had several driveways and entrances, was for the first time integrated with the pattern of the surrounding landscape. Nothing is known of any specific iconographical programme for the garden, where the vertical accent supplied by the narrow obelisks dominates the general impression.

PROBLEMS OF CONSERVATION   What has been the fate of the terraced gardens in Central Europe I have been describing?

Of Matthias Corvinus' *giardino pensile* on Buda's Castle Hill nothing remains, except for the *cisterna regia*. The castle garden was transferred later from the west side of the hill to the more attractive Danube side. Between 1875 and 1882 the architect Miklós Ybl created the so-called 'Castle Garden Bazar' in

4

Budapest, a luxuriously constructed area of ornamental terraces with various pavilions in the style of the Viennese Neo-Renaissance.[17] Whether or not Ybl was inspired by the glorious Corvinian era of the late fifteenth century cannot be stated with certainty, although a somewhat Mediterranean character in the original historicist proposals for planting the garden suggests that this might have been the case. Today the condition of the Castle Garden Bazar is truly awful; the Communists having used parts of the building for many years as a 'Youth Park' with a discothèque, this marvellous piece of architecture is now little better than a ruin.

In Visegrád (Hungary) the terraced palace and gardens of Matthias Corvinus were mostly excavated after the Second World War and parts of them conserved or reconstructed.[18] In the main courtyard the foundation of the fountain has been secured and an impression of its original aspect re-created by placing a marble cover with reliefs over it. The terraces are today completely bare of the plantation which existed here in the time of Matthias, although research into this is now beginning.

The present aspect of what was once the garden of the Neugebäude in Vienna is no less depressing than that of the nineteenth-century castle in Budapest.[19] As previously mentioned, Emperor Rudolph II had no interest in bringing the bold plans of his predecessor to fruition. The gardens were still being cultivated, albeit in a more modest form, around 1600; finally they fell into ruin during the reign of Maria Theresia, when the Neugebäude became a powder store for the military. Although the whole complex was still being adequately cared for in the first half of the seventeenth century, and although the architect Fischer von Erlach was still planning its revival around 1700 and the architect Hohenberg reused many interesting fragments of it in the imperial garden of Schönbrunn, by the end of the eighteenth century few knew or cared about the significance of this Renaissance garden.

Around 1985 the Neugebäude became an issue in the local politics of Vienna and ambitious plans were aired for its restoration. The 11th District of Vienna, an area between the airport and the old city that possessed no notable sight other than the Central Cemetery, was to be given new dignity through the resurrection of the 'Renaissance Castle'. The estimated cost of the project was about a billion schillings. The plan included restoration or reconstruction of the gardens.

Of this grandiose project, which has subsequently run into the sand, only the very first phase, consisting of the research into historical data and preliminary discussions as to methodology, was completed.[20] In Leiden in 1990 I reported on these debates and discussions and pointed out that the avail-

4 Neuwaldegg today (1995).
(Photo: Géza Hajós)

5

able written and pictorial sources were insufficient to carry out, for example, an exact reconstruction of the flower-beds in the northern flower-garden. In this respect we drew upon the expertise of Mrs. Oldenburger-Ebbers and suggested that an attempt be made at a 're-performance' of the garden complex, in the sense associated with the late Professor Jörg Gamer.[21] The excavations supplied useful information on the architectonic spaces and on the foundations for the fountains and the pools. On the other hand, pollen archaeology failed to come up with anything worthwhile on the flowers originally planted. The Horticultural Department of the City of Vienna made an experimental flower-bed in the manner of Sebastiano Serlio;[22] only later did the garden books of Hans Puechfeldner, dedicated in 1592-93 to the emperor Rudolph II in Prague, become known.[23]

Much less discussed at that time was the integration of the garden reconstruction into the present landscape, which is of course vastly different from that of the sixteenth and seventeenth centuries. At present, the northern flower-garden is framed by new housing estates and even the view of the Danube is obstructed by several industrial buildings. It was only later that students of the University of Agriculture in Vienna, taking part in a competition, attempted to resolve this complex situation in terms of ecological town planning. However, as already stated, all these deliberations have been put on ice for the time being.

THE BELVEDERE   On the other hand, the Federal Office of Historic Monuments in Austria commissioned plans a few years ago for the restoration of the Belvedere garden in Vienna, which, despite all the changes in the nineteenth century, still retained its late-baroque character.[24] In the context of these plans, the original geometric design of the early eighteenth century was regarded as fundamental to restoration, as the changes to the garden could not be regarded as significant examples of the taste of a later epoch. In the lower area of bosquets, the Administration of Federal Gardens in Austria carried out a pruning exercise that went back to the 'Delsenbach plan' (fig. 5).[25] However, the figures in the central walkway – which originally stood on the top of the orangery and were brought here in the time of Peter Krafft, director of the Picture Gallery in the Belvedere – remained, of course, in their nineteenth-century positions. In the central parterre area, the parterres with flower-bordure were reconstructed

5 The bosquet area of the Belvedere in Vienna, situation in 1990. (Photo: Géza Hajós)

6 The reconstructed parterres at the Belvedere in Vienna. (Photo: Géza Hajós)

7

in the manner of the late eighteenth century (fig. 6); the broderies from the time of Prince Eugene were not reconstituted.

There are still numerous problems with the Belvedere: the water supply has decayed (two new wells would be necessary), the condition of much of the garden sculpture and the steps gives cause for concern, as does the brutal asphalting of the paths undertaken in the fifties. In planning the latest restoration of both Belvedere palaces for museum purposes, the responsible ministry refused to consider the garden as an integral part of the restoration.

It is also important to realize that the role played by the Belvedere garden in the city's panorama underwent a fundamental change during the founder period (the *Gründerzeit* in the second half of the nineteenth century). Tall apartment houses dominate the scene that once inspired Canaletto. A storey has already been removed from one of the houses; nevertheless modern hotels rise in the middle distance, and destroy the illusion that one is enjoying the same view as that which so gratified and flattered Prince Eugene.

However, due to the fact that so much is preserved of the whole and that so many authentic architectonic riches are to hand, the Belvedere garden can be regarded as a self-defining aesthetic unit and can therefore be treated independently of the changes that have marked its immediate surroundings. The garden is a priceless gem in a late-twentieth-century metropolis in Central Europe and should be preserved and maintained accordingly.

SCHLOSSHOFF More difficult is the problem of conservation of the baroque garden at Schlosshof in Lower Austria (figs. 7 and 8): on the one hand, restorers are confronted with the fact that there has been a massive reduction of its original sculptural and architectonic riches, particularly since the First World War; on the other, they have had to recognize that the most recent excavations have produced unexpected results in terms of, for example, foundations and ground colouring.[26] Some 70 per cent of the garden sculpture has been lost, but against this can be set the equally large number of garden constructions that have been discovered through excavation (water-pipes, steps, embankments, foundations for pavilions, flower-bed structures, etc.). The archaeologists are in favour of a total reconstruction, since without protective measures – which would strongly influence or even destroy the overall picture of the baroque garden – the finds cannot be left uncovered and are thus in the long term unsuitable as a public attraction. The art historians warn against attempting a total reconstruction, since the missing sculptures cannot be replaced and modern reconstructions of the pavilions would have doubtful

8

7 Antonio Canaletto. *A View of the Terraces at Schlosshof*. Detail. Kunsthistorisches Museum, Vienna. (Photo: Géza Hajós)

8 The terraced gardens at Schlosshof, situation in 1990. (Photo: Géza Hajós)

authenticity. The gardeners warn of the cost that would be involved in maintenance, without which there is no point in embarking on complicated projects for vegetation. The three Canaletto paintings seem to provide a good basis for determining what form the reconstruction should take, although in this case there are no surviving written sources supplying concrete evidence. The Federal Office of Historic Monuments in Austria must tread a delicate path through all these conflicting views and inhibiting factors.

On several terraces the lines of trees have been replanted in conformity with the historical evidence: in these areas the vegetation was not only exhausted, but was itself the result of alterations in the nineteenth century. Two trees were allowed to remain, since these may be regarded as examples of deliberate aesthetic renewal dating from the late nineteenth century. In general, one can say that, apart from some vegetation introduced subsequent to the baroque period, no new aesthetic concept was applied and one therefore can speak of a progressive decay as far as the trees were concerned. For this reason one can happily support the idea of renewing them, without thereby totally closing off the possibility of a more abundant reconstruction of the vegetation as well. As a result of archaeological research, one may already now (and will in the future be able to) re-create the slopes and banks in their correct positions and angles, since these also had been moved or become deformed over the centuries. The basins of the fountains could also be given priority in the restoration programme, and even, in the last resort, be completely reconstructed. The reconstruction of the grid of pathways has so far not been embarked upon, due to the lack of available staff for maintenance. In general, one can say that things have recently begun to move at Schlosshof; however, due to the current need for drastic savings in the state budget, the debate over future plans is still very much alive.

SCHLOSS WALDEGG The situation in Switzerland was different as regards Schloss Waldegg. Archaeological excavations were also carried out here; on the basis of these findings, a complete reconstruction of the southern garden terrace was boldly undertaken. The 1984 declaration by the authorities concerning the garden read as follows: 'The aim of the measures to be financed with requisite credits is to reconstruct the ornamental parterre south of the main building as a focal point of the baroque garden, without thereby endangering the great trees planted in the previous century. The latter shall be preserved as long as they remain healthy and do not endanger the surrounding walls or disturb the overall aspect of the castle.'[27] However, the nineteenth-century aspect of the park was in the end sacrificed for the sake of this reconstruction, even though it could be shown to be based on an individual and novel aesthetic. It was felt that the requirements of environmental conservation would have been met if the south *allée* (an important factor in the integration of landscape that was lost in the nineteenth century), was replanted with one hundred lime-trees. Instead of re-creating the ornamental borders in all their original richness, simple areas of lawn were laid out. For these areas the obelisks and the southern steps with fountains were rebuilt from scratch. One gets the impression that the Swiss public wanted, almost at any price, to be reassured that sumptuous baroque gardens have also existed in Switzerland.

As far as the Neuwaldegg garden in Vienna is concerned, a complete reconstruction is not considered appropriate, although it is tempting to think that the 1719 print mentioned above supplies a suitable model for it (fig. 3). Archaeological research in this region would certainly yield some intriguing information. The provisional decision of the Federal Office of Historic Monuments in Austria, however, requires that the so-called 'state of cultivation' be conserved, by which is meant the baroquization of the late nineteenth century together with its scheme of plantation.[28]

The landscape perspective of the Neuwaldegg baroque garden has been radically altered by the building of a 1950s apartment house immediately in front of the last terrace, which, of course, cannot be demolished. The existence of the house also justifies the decision to accept the changes of later epochs in the case of this particular garden complex, and not to pursue the *fata morgana* of a total reconstruction which, in truth, would have rather more to do with wishful thinking than with an authentic reconstruction after which the experts hanker (fig. 4).

Historic gardens, including terraced gardens, retain their authenticity only when their historical development is also taken into account. Of course that does not mean that the elements of *every* period have to be conserved or emphasized.

Translated from the German by Nicholas Parsons

---

1 Feuerné-Tóth, 'A budai vár függőkertje és a Cisterna Regia', pp. 11-54.
2 Scamozzi, *L'idea della architettura universale*, p. 348; Balogh, *A muveszet Matyas király udvarában*, p. 91.
3 Feuerné-Tóth, 'A budai vár függőkertje és a Cisterna Regia', p. 50; Hegedüs, *Analecta Nova*, p. 56.
4 Balogh, 'Die Kunst der Renaissance in Ungarn', p. 87.
5 Hajós, 'Renaissance Gardens in Austria', pp. 85-95.
6 Eisler, *Das barocke Wien*, p. 75 (no. 298, plate 229).
7 Hajós, 'Neuwaldegg – der älteste Garten «nach englischer Art» in Österreich', pp. 109-44.
8 d'Aviler, *Cours d'Architecture*.
9 Hans Aurenhammer, 'Der Garten des Prinzen Eugen'; Hans and Gertrude Aurenhammer, *Das Belvedere in Wien*.
10 Maurer, *Geschichte des k.k. Lustschlosses Schlosshof*;
Madritsch, 'Zur Geschichte und Restaurierung von Schlosshof in den Jahren 1984-1985', pp. 76-86.
11 Aurenhammer, *Das Belvedere in Wien*.
12 Hajós, *Romantische Gärten der Aufklärung*; see especially the chapter 'Vom glorreichen Belvedere zur romantischen Aussicht', pp. 15-26.
13 Schmidt, 'Belvedere', pp. 241-49, after Aurenhammer.
14 Until now we have no scientific article on the iconological programme of Schlosshof. Dr. Peter Konig (Bundesdenkmalamt Wien) is working on these problems.
15 The three Schlosshof paintings by Canaletto are in the Kunsthistorisches Museum, Vienna.
16 Carlen, *Schloss Waldegg bei Solothurn*.
17 *Budapest müemlékei*, 1, pp. 742-43.
18 Dercsenyi, *Visegrád müemlékei*.

19 Hajós, 'Renaissance Gardens in Austria'.
20 Unfortunately, the scientific results of the research team under the leadership of Professor Manfred Wehdorn (Vienna, Technical University) are not published.
21 Professor Gamer used the German word *Wiederaufführung*. The English authors Mavis Collier and David Wrightson use the notion 're-creation' in this context; see Collier and Wrigthson, 'The Re-creation of the Turkish Tent at Painshill', pp. 50-51. See also Sigel, 'Der gewachsene und der rekonstruierte Garten', pp. 341-46.
22 The first experiments with the reconstruction of a Renaissance flower-bed after Matthäus Merian (1649) were not successful. This illustration is the earliest engraving from the south side of the Neugebäude, but it is inexact.
23 Dr. Erik de Jong, Free University, Amsterdam is preparing a monograph on Hans Puechfeldner (to be published with Dumbarton Oaks, Washington, DC).
24 Auböck and Schmidt, *Schloss Belvedere Wien*, pp. 168-86.
25 This marvellous plan is published in *Die Gartenkunst*, 1992, no. 2, pp. 169-71.
26 Auböck and Schmidt, *Schlosshof – Vorgutachten*; Sauer, 'Gartenarchäologie in Schlosshof', pp. 134-42.
27 Carlen, *Schloss Waldegg bei Solothurn*, p. 228.
28 Zbiral, *Schloss Neuwaldegg Wien*; Zbiral, 'Neuwaldegg', in *Historische Gärten*, pp. 283-87.

....

Auböck, Maria, and Stefan Schmidt. *Schlosshof – Vorgutachten Gartendenkmalpflege.* Manuscript in Bundesdenkmalamt Wien (Federal Office of Historic Monuments, Vienna), 1991.

Auböck, Maria, and Stefan Schmidt. *Schloss Belvedere Wien – Konzept zur Restaurierung des Gartenkomplexes.* Management Plan. Manuscript in the archives of the Bundesdenkmalamt Wien, 1992.

Aurenhammer, Hans. 'Der Garten des Prinzen Eugen'. In *Mitteilungen der Österreichischen Galerie*, Sonderheft 'Prinz Eugen und sein Belvedere'. Vienna, 1963.

Aurenhammer, Hans and Gertrude. *Das Belvedere in Wien.* Vienna, 1971.

d'Aviler, Charles. *Cours d'Architecture.* 2 vols. Paris, 1691.

Balogh, Jolán. *A muveszet Matyas király udvarában (Art at the Court of King Matthias).* Budapest, 1966.

Balogh, Jolán. 'Die Kunst der Renaissance in Ungarn'. In *Matthias Corvinus und die Renaissance in Ungarn 1458-1541.* Schallaburg, 1982.

'Budapest müemlékei, I (Historic Monuments of Budapest, I)'. In *Magyarország muemléki topógrafiája, IV. kötet.* Budapest, 1955, pp. 742-43.

Carlen, Georg (ed.). *Schloss Waldegg bei Solothurn (Château de Waldegg près de Soleure).* Solothurn: Aare-Verlag, 1991.

Collier, M., and D. Wrigthson. 'The Re-creation of the Turkish Tent at Painshill'. In *Garden History*, 21 (1993), 1, pp. 50-51.

Dercsenyi, Dezso. *Visegrád müemlékei (Historic Monuments of Visegrád).* Budapest, 1951.

Eisler, Max. *Das barocke Wien.* Vienna / Leipzig, 1925.

Feuerné-Tóth, Rozsa. 'A budai vár függökertje és a Cisterna Regia (The «hanging gardens» of the Castle in Buda and the «Cisterna Regia»)'. In *Magyarorszgi reneszansz es barokk.* MTA Müvesztürténeti Kutatócsoport kiadványai. Budapest: Akadémiai Kiadó, 1975, pp. 11-54.

Hajós, Géza. 'Neuwaldegg – der älteste Garten «nach englischer Art» in Österreich'. In *Wiener Jahrbuch für Kunstgeschichte*, XXXIX (1986), pp. 109-44.

Hajós, Géza. *Romantische Gärten der Aufklärung – englische Landschaftskultur des 18. Jahrhunderts in und um Wien.* Cologne, 1989.

Hajós, Géza. 'Renaissance Gardens in Austria. Current Research Findings and Perspectives for Conservation'. In L. Tjon Sie Fat and E. de Jong, *The Authentic Garden.* Leiden: Clusius Foundation, 1991, pp. 85-95.

Hegedüs, Abel-. *Analecta Nova ad Historiam Renascentium.* Budapest, 1903.

Historische Gärten in Österreich. Vienna / Cologne / Weimar: Österreichische Gesellschaft für historische Gärten, 1993.

Madritsch, Renate. 'Zur Geschichte und Restaurierung von Schlosshof in den Jahren 1984-1985'. In *Österreichische Zeitschrift fur Kunst und Denkmalpflege*, XL (1986), pp. 76-86.

Maurer, Joseph. *Geschichte des k. k. Lustschlosses Schlosshof.* Vienna, 1889.

Sauer, Franz. 'Gartenarchäologie in Schlosshof'. In *Die Gartenkunst*, 1995, no. 1, pp. 134-42.

Scamozzi, Vicenzo. *L'idea della architettura universale.* Venice, 1694.

Schmidt, Stefan. 'Parkpflegewerk Belvedere-Garten in Wien'. In *Die Gartenkunst*, 1992, no. 2, pp. 168-86.

Schmidt, Stefan. 'Belvedere'. In *Historische Gärten in Österreich.* Vienna / Cologne / Weimar: Österreichische Gesellschaft für historische Gärten, 1993, pp. 241-49.

Sigel, Brigitt. 'Der gewachsene und der rekonstruierte Garten. Gedanken anlässlich zweier Tagungen über Gartenarchäologie'. In *Die Gartenkunst*, 1995, no. 2, pp. 341-46.

Zbiral, Andreas. *Schloss Neuwaldegg Wien – Gutachten zur Gartendenkmalpflege.* Manuscript in Bundesdenkmalamt Wien, 1993.

Zbiral, Andreas. 'Neuwaldegg'. In *Historische Gärten in Österreich.* Vienna / Cologne / Weimar: Österreichische Gesellschaft für historische Gärten, 1993, pp. 283-87.

The restoration of seventeenth- and eighteenth-century gardens and cultural landscapes in Sweden

KJELL LUNDQUIST

THE RESTORATION AND maintenance of gardens, parks and designed landscapes in an informed and scientific manner, preceded by documentation and formulation of aims in accordance with the requirements of the Florence Charter (1981) or similar documents, is a comparatively new feature in Sweden.[1] An exception, however, is the attention given to the cultural landscape, in its broadest sense.

This does not mean, however, that restoration work in gardens, of different sorts and to different degrees, is not carried out, or is unknown in Sweden. This work, however, has had more of a renewing, or rationalizing, architectural character, rather than being actual restoration work in the term's modern sense. Mostly, this has concerned gardens continually in use by their owners, that is to say not 'preserved monuments', and it may thus be difficult to tell whether a feature of a garden in the historical perspective is the result of an earlier premeditated restoration effort, or just an 'add-on' inspired by contemporary ideals. When, for example, in the 1730s, Carl Hårleman (1700-1753) redesigned the royal gardens at Ekolsund near Lake Mälaren in mid-Sweden, he tactfully preserved the then out-of-fashion ornamental parterres put there by his father, Johan Hårleman (1662-1707), and instead gave them a new context.

RESTORING SWEDISH GARDENS Few Swedish landscape architects have worked exclusively with restoration of historical parks and gardens during this century. The works of Walter Bauer (1912-1994), landscape architect and fellow of the Royal Academy of Fine Arts, epitomize the concept in Sweden. His first restoration project, at the end of the 1940s, concerned the garden of Gunnebo Manor, south of Göteborg, designed in 1780-90 by Carl Wilhelm Carlberg. Its strict classicist design is considered to be one of the most genuine examples of an eighteenth-century garden in Sweden. Carlberg's commission included the design of the entire estate, from the siting of the buildings in the surrounding landscape, to the master plan of the garden, down to the design of the greenhouse pots. The garden has been restored, keeping as closely as possible to the original plans.

1

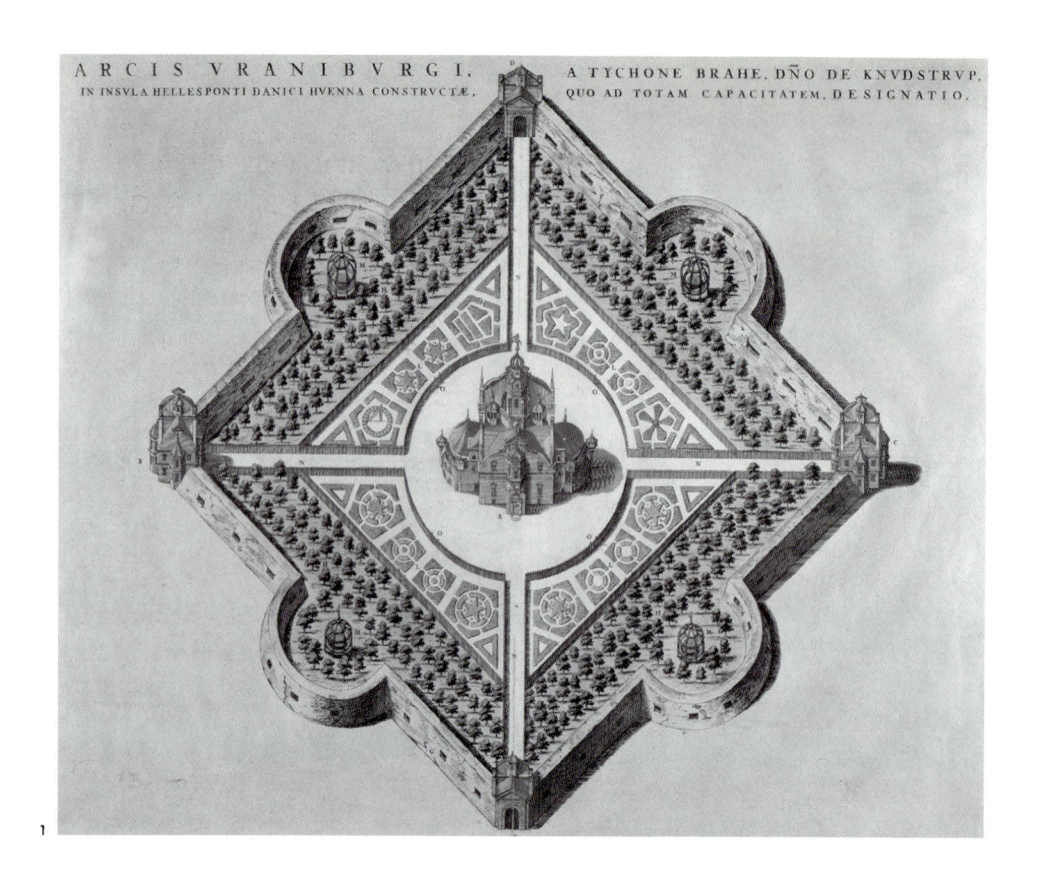

2a

1 Plan of Tycho Brahe's garden at Uraniborg, Island of Ven, from the 1580s, published in J. Blaeu, *Atlas Maior*, T. 1, Europa, Liber II, Amsterdam, 1662 (University Library Lund. Photo: UB-Media, Lund)

2 Views of the reconstructed garden at Uraniborg, Island of Ven, in 1994. (Photos: Kjell Lundquist, 1994)

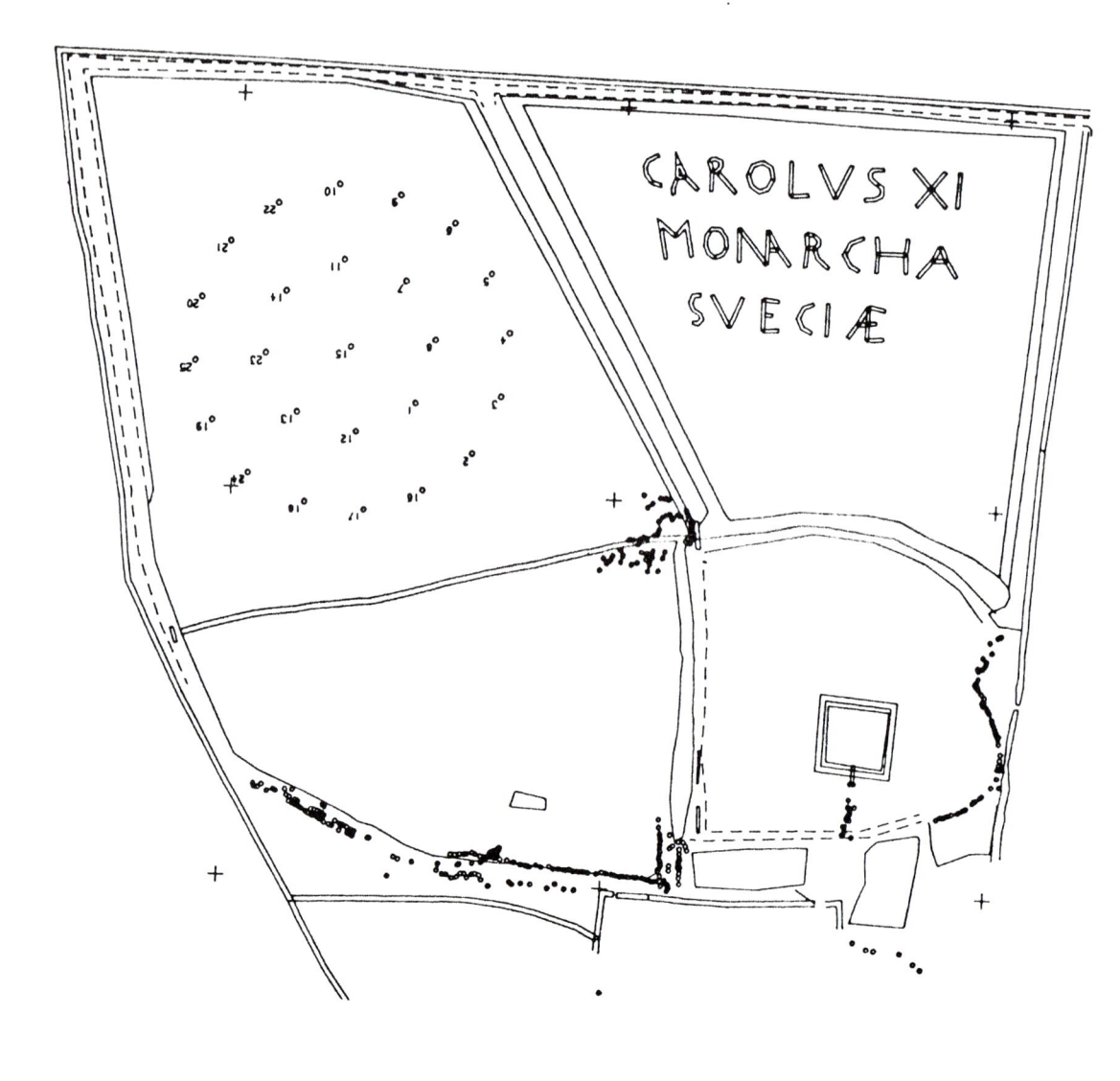

Bauer's most prominent restoration project, which was carried out over an extended period of time, concerned the Royal Palace of Drottningholm, near Stockholm, with its baroque garden and landscaped park. The foundations of Drottningholm were laid in 1662 according to drawings by Nicodemus Tessin the Elder. The baroque garden was first laid in 1682 according to new designs by his son, Nicodemus Tessin the Younger. Of great importance to the plantations and maintenance of the garden was Johan Hårleman, master gardener at Drottningholm from 1692, and son of Christian Horleman, who was summoned from Holland to Sweden by Queen Hedvig Eleonora. In the years 1680-85 Johan Hårleman made his grand tour of Europe, including a visit to Holland. He returned to Holland in 1699-70, partly in order to purchase plants. Bauer's contribution includes restoration/renovation of the various parterres, hedges and bosquet arrangements. Drottningholm is now the residence of the Swedish Royal Family and one of the Swedish sites on the UNESCO World Heritage List.

Other large and important parks and gardens of stately homes in Sweden completely or partly restored by Walter Bauer include Ulriksdal and Rosersberg near Stockholm, Strömholm by Nicodemus Tessin the Elder, in central Sweden, and the early industrial estates of Forsmark, Leufsta and Engelsberg. Engelsberg is now also being proposed for the World Heritage List. The restored sites are documented in Bauer's book *Parker, Trädgådar och landskap – förnya och bevara* (Parks, Gardens and Landscapes – to Renew and to Preserve) (1990). The influence of Walter Bauer on the restoration of historical gardens in Sweden during the past fifty years has been significant – both by virtue of the examples he has created and by his methodology and approach. The point of departure has been mainly that of the consulting architect, the intuitive method and the preference often given to the formal garden.

RECENT PROJECTS   Some of the more interesting and most scrupulous restoration projects of sixteenth-, seventeenth- and eighteenth-century gardens and cultural landscapes in Sweden today include the Renaissance gardens of Uraniborg on the island of Ven between Sweden and Denmark, Östra Sallerup in southern Sweden, the Baroque Garden of Drottningholm and the landscape around Råshult, in Småland, the birthplace and childhood home of Carl von Linné.

Uraniborg, at that time part of Denmark (Ven became Swedish in 1658), was created by the renowned Danish astronomer and nobleman Tycho Brahe (1546-1601) (figs.1 and 2a-c). Its strict, symmetrical garden, based on the square and the circle – as a celestial projection on Earth of the divine geometry – was laid out in the 1580s. The restoration of the garden, initiated in 1985 and based among other sources on archaeological excavations in 1988-92, has had Professor Sven-Ingvar Andersson of Copenhagen as the aesthetic supervisor. Two keywords apply to the restoration work: 'partial reconstruction', referring to the fact that only a quarter of the ornamental garden and ramparts has been rebuilt; and 'planting hypothesis', to reflect the tentativeness of the selection and grouping of the plant material. In an ongoing project, the plantations are being developed to replace all plants with species which can be verified as having occurred in late-sixteenth-century Denmark, or on Ven.

Östra Sallerup is a peculiar Renaissance garden consisting of four large quarters roughly 200 by 200 metres, with the character of a walled copse of deciduous trees, out in the middle of the Scanian countryside (fig.3). It was

3 Plan of the Priest's garden at Östra Sallerup (second half of the seventeenth century) after a survey done in 1993.

4

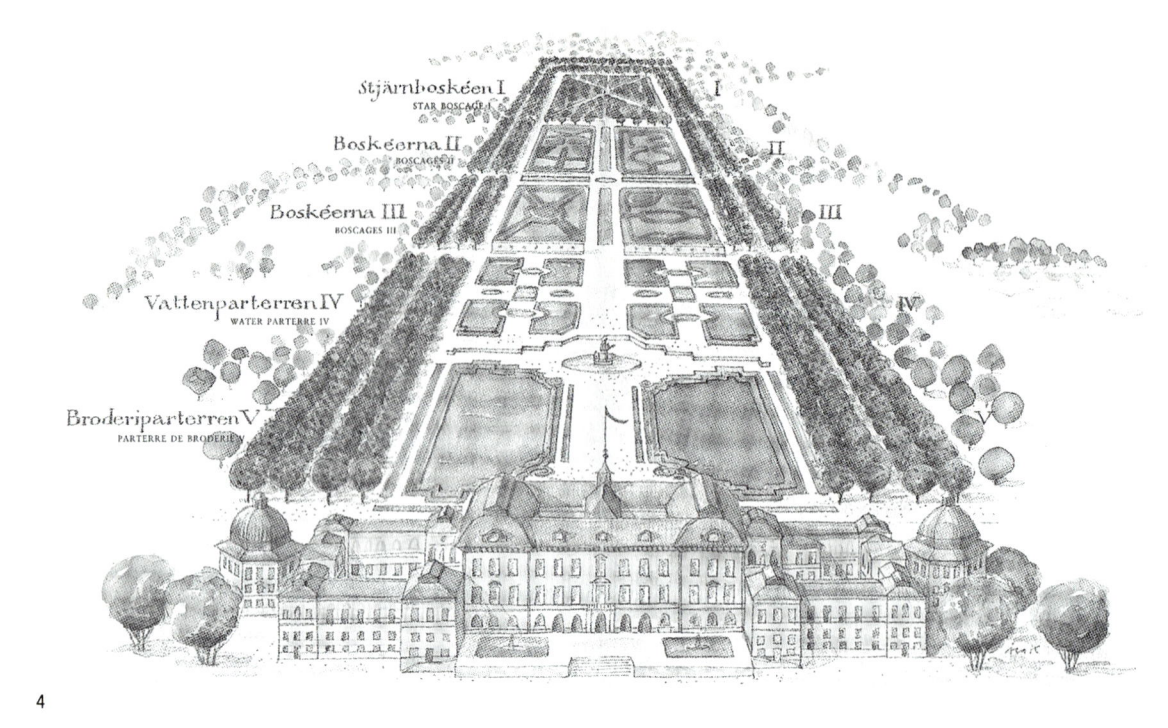

created in the second half of the seventeenth century, when Scania became part of Sweden, under the auspices of the clergyman Jöns Hendriksson. Documentation and restoration work, including archaeological excavations, have been carried out since 1990. Many questions still remain to be answered – why, for instance, was the garden created, whence came its inspiration and how were the construction work and ensuing maintenance financed?

At Drottningholm, the main issue is how to achieve a rejuvenation of the double rows of linden around the baroque garden, about eight hundred trees in all, including several individuals of the so-called Dutch linden planted in the 1680s, in the times of Nicodemus Tessin the Younger (figs. 4 and 5). How can historic authenticity be preserved after three hundred years of additions and replacements and how can the genetic stock be carried forward? The possibility of restoring the ornamental parterres, also from the 1680s, in close proximity to the palace building, is also being discussed. The source material is comparatively rich in information. Erik Dahlberg's detailed copperplate engravings in his *Suecia antiqua et hodierna* (1661-1713), in particular, provide a vivid collection of images.

Around Råshult, the Central Board of National Antiquities is allocating considerable resources to restoring a substantial area of small-scale eighteenth-century agricultural landscape, with its physical structure formed by the traditional elements of small fenced crop-fields, stone walls, hayfields, woodland grazing, coppiced trees and kitchen gardens. The aim of this restoration effort is to recreate both the spatial characteristics and the biological contents of the rural landscape of Carl von Linné's childhood, based on his own descriptions of the countryside.

Some other interesting restoration projects include Carl Hårleman's Lundagård in Lund, Fredrik Magnus Piper's landscape park from the 1780s at Haga in Stockholm – the aforementioned Gunnebo and Fredriksdal Manor (1850) in Helsingborg, south Sweden. At Gunnebo and Fredriksdal, the old kitchen gardens are currently the focus of the restoration efforts. Tyresö Manor, near Stockholm, is being completely renovated for about 35 million Swedish crowns. The Swedish Minister for Cultural Affairs has pledged that the landscape garden will be included in the scheme.

In many places around the country, work with, and in, several other seventeenth- and eighteenth-century gardens is going on, more or less unnoticed.

5

4 Scheme of the garden at Drottningholm, showing the different phases of replanting, beginning at the far end (the west side) of the garden: phase I (200 trees) in 1997, phase II (176 trees) in 2002, phase III (112 trees) in 2010, phase IV (160 trees) in 2015 and phase V (144 trees) in 2020. (Photo after *The Renewal of Drottningholm's Avenue of Limes*, The National Properties Board, 1996)

5 The north avenue of limes (Tilia x Vulgaris) in the garden at Drottningholm. (Photo: Rune Bengtsson 1994)

We still know very little about what is actually happening to our historical garden heritage. Swedish authorities have so far not quite managed the task of identifying and listing our historical parks and gardens according to article 23 of the Florence Charter.

THE CULTURAL LANDSCAPE   If preservation, management and restoration of historical parks and gardens took their time to reach the top of the agenda, the cultural landscape, in its broadest sense, tells a different story. Strangely enough, this is largely a result of early Swedish nature conservation concerns and the development of nature conservation legislation in Sweden. Already in 1880, only eight years after the founding of the first national park in the world, Yellowstone in the United States, advanced discussions were being held in Sweden concerning national parks. The first Nature Conservation Act came

6

into effect in 1909, and at the same time the first nine of the present 23 national parks in Sweden were established. These 23 parks comprise 6,300 hectares of land and a further 16,200 hectares is being considered.

The national parks were mostly laid out in areas of 'untouched' land, to protect the natural flora and wildlife. An interesting and instructive exception is Dalby Söderskog, the first national park in Scania, dating from 1918 and consisting of 30 hectares of deciduous woodland, then believed to be a virgin forest residue of the Scanian plains. It is indubitably a very beautiful and attractive place, well worth preserving, with its many glades and grand old oak trees, but is in fact, according to more recent findings, a cultural vestige. Swedish nature reserves, on the other hand (established following the Nature Conservation Act of 1964 and today attaining to approximately 27,000 square kilometres), more often have a culture-based rationale. Among them we find not only meadows and pastures, areas of former woodland grazing, groves and mosaic landscapes, but also areas with more architectural elements such as tree rows, clumps and landscape gardens. Under Swedish nature conservation legislation, some areas are even protected for the specifically aesthetic qualities of the landscape.

This partly 'unintentional' protection that the land around many estates and other old cultural environments has received as a result of nature conservation aspirations has had, as far as this author is able to see, a profound influence on the preservation of our historical garden heritage. That legislation concerning the cultural heritage should be so much weaker than that concerning nature conservation is, of course, highly unsatisfactory. One should be grateful, though, for the disguised or coincidental protection of aesthetic and cultural values which has followed from considerations mainly devoted to issues of nature conservation. A good example of this is the extensive system of avenues in the landscape around the manor house of Övedskloster (1760-70) in Scania (fig. 6). This has been designated a natural monument, although both its origin and its rationale are purely aesthetic and functional and the trees clearly a culture-induced addition to the landscape. One may note that of the 175 historical gardens in Sweden protected under the Act concerning Ancient Monuments and Finds, according to which management plans are mandatory, only four have such plans, among them Vrams Gunnarstorp (from the seventeenth century) in Scania – whereas almost all of the nature conservation areas have had management plans prepared for them.

Due to the early awakening of nature conservation awareness and the relative abundance of sparsely populated nature areas, forced restoration of cultural landscapes has never really been necessary in Sweden – it has mostly been

6 Sigfried Rålamb's view of Övedskloster, c.1790. (Rålamb Collection, Royal Library, Stockholm)

possible to protect the values of the cultural landscapes within the framework of the nature reserves' management schemes.

The wealth of Swedish garden history lies, as I see it, not in grand, modern and scientific, detailed restorations of individual parterres or other specific park compounds, but more in the abundance of less well-known, yet more or less historic, seventeenth- and eighteenth-century parks and gardens in the country. They have, with a few exceptions, suffered relatively limited modifications, and may well serve as reference objects for future restoration projects. Above all, Sweden can boast a richness on the landscape scale, a relatively unspoiled countryside which is the setting of the historical sites and provides them with a wider context. Ulfåsa in mid-Sweden, Övedskloster and Maltesholm in Scania, are but a few examples of gardens where the consciously refined surrounding landscape is still there to be seen.

If I am forced to choose: the elements of a landscape – the tree rows, the orchards and kitchen gardens, the pleasure gardens, the fields, the pastures, groves, copses and woodlands, as well as the buildings – may well be run down, derelict, unkempt or disused, but one should provide that there remains a prevailing 'ambiance of the structural wholeness', that special quality of a place that conveys a deeper understanding of all the activities in fields, forests and at sea. These founded the capital whose interest furnished the pleasure gardens in the first place. The surrounding countryside should, in the words of Professor Erik Lundberg (1930), be big enough for one to sense the 'life-style and spirit of times long gone by' – which is also the essence of the Florence Charter Articles. The challenges for restoration in Sweden, therefore, lie above all in the future, and in the task of preserving the wider contexts of these productive as well as enjoyable landscapes.

Owing to unforeseen circumstances, we were unable to publish Kjell Lundquist's lecture in full.

---

1 A symposium on this subject was, however, staged at the Swedish Agricultural University at Alnarp, 21-23 September 1994. Its papers have now been published; they give a good perspective on the state of art where garden restoration in Sweden is concerned. See Bonnier, Ann Catherine and Kjell Lundquist, *Historiska parker och trädgårdar – ett arv att vårda och sköta. Rapport fran ett seminarium pa Alnarp 21-23 september 1994*, Stockholm: Riksantikvarieämbetet, 1996, with further literature. See also the regular contributions to *Lustgården. Yearbook of the Swedish Society for Dendrology and Parkculture.*

The restoration of the gardens of Sigiriya, Sri Lanka

NILAN COORAY

THE INTENTION OF this paper is to explain in brief the spatial organization of the Sigiriya gardens, which are among the oldest surviving gardens of the ancient world, and to outline the conservation work being done under the UNESCO-Sri Lanka Project of the Cultural Triangle.

Located at a site of incomparable natural beauty, Sigiriya was the centre of government and court life of Sri Lanka for a brief period of eighteen years in the fifth century AD, when the 'radical' king Kasyapa (477-495) shifted the capital to Sigiriya from the then established capital of Anuradhapura. The most remarkable aspect of Sigiriya is that it is one of the best preserved and most elaborate surviving cities of the fifth century AD[1] in Asia, with a unique concentration of town planning, art and architecture, landscape gardening, hydraulic and military engineering.[2] The city is centred upon a monumental rock, which rises with sheer cliffs on all sides to a height of 165 metres above the surrounding plain (fig.1). The royal palace complex is situated at the summit of the rock, about 1.5 hectares in extent. To the east and west, below the rock, there is a series of precincts fortified by moats and ramparts.

Axial planning seems to have been the most characteristic feature of the landscape of the Sigiriya region, with its north-south and east-west axes intersecting at the midpoint of the central rock (fig.2). Along the north-south axis lie the ancient Buddhist monastery of Pidurangala to the north and the great man-made Sigiriya tank to the south of the city. The agricultural settlements of the population with their irrigation tanks, which are typical of Sri Lankan dry-zone settlement patterns, are situated outside the northern walls of the city. Beyond the southern city walls is another fortified rocky site (a garrison?), bordering the Sigiriya tank bund to the west. This site had a direct link with the central hilly terrain of the city, through the top of the tank bund. An iron-producing site to the farther south of the north-south axis has also been discovered, indicating a possible 'industrial' zone.

As regards the Sigiriya city proper, the topography of its outer compounds is virtually flat, while the area immediately below the rock gradually climbs towards the rock's base, which gives a skirting effect to the unscalable rock from the plain below. The somewhat elliptical-shaped outer limits of this sloping terrain are enclosed by a wall forming an inner royal precinct, with its main gateway facing west. Beyond this to the east and west, on the plain below, are two rectangular precincts, fortified by wide moats and high earthen ramparts (fig. 4). Encompassing all these precincts, together with the central rock, is another large rectangular enclosure (an outer city?), the limits of which are again defined by a moat and a rampart. Essentially, the whole city of Sigiriya is oriented along its east-west axis, which gradually appears from the distant dense jungle to the west, runs across the fortified precincts and bisects the north-south oriented rock, and eventually disappears again in the green canopies of the jungles to the east. The overall layout of Sigiriya is symmetrical in relation to this axis, with eastern and western city gateways directly aligned with it.

1 *The gardens of Sigiriya*

The famous gardens of Sigiriya, whose fifth-century layout and other features are still in a fair state of preservation, lie to the west of the north-south axis, occupying both the western rectangular precinct and the western slopes of the inner royal precinct. The western precinct is designed for the pleasures of the royal family. The east-west axial pathway divides the whole garden into two identical sectors, with elaborate pavilions surrounded by water, reflecting

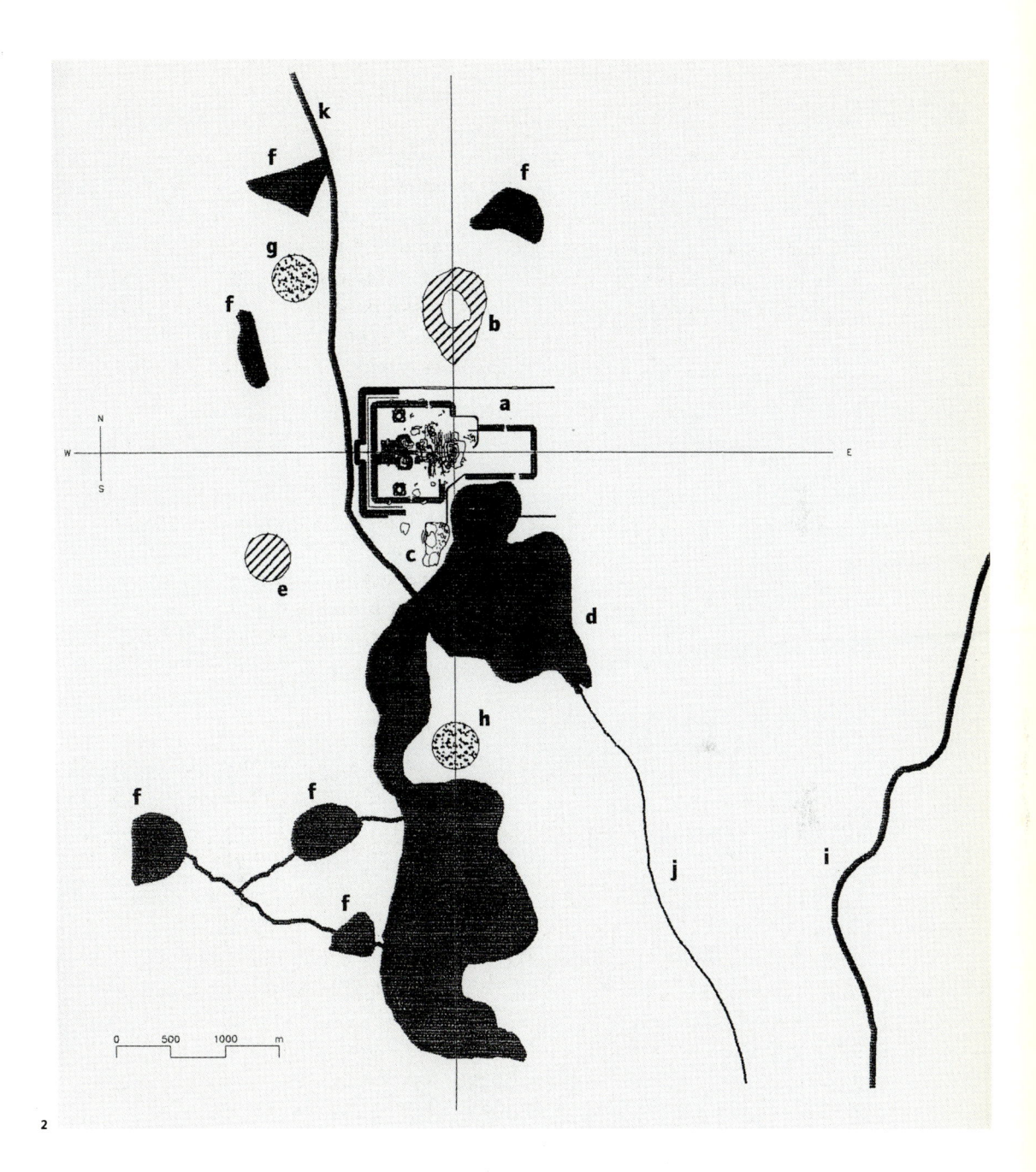

1 The rock of Sigiriya towering above the rest of the landscape. (Photo: Nilan Cooray)
2 Plan of the 'greater Sigiriya' with the tanks, Mapagala fortifications, monasteries, settlements, etc.

a *Sigiriya city*
b *Pidurangala monastery*
c *Mapagala fortifications*
d *Sigiriya tank*
e *Ramakele monastery*
f *Tank*
g *Ancient settlement*
h *Ancient iron-producing site*
i *Kiri-oya (stream)*
j *Supply canal from Kiri-oya*
k *Sigiri-oya (stream)*

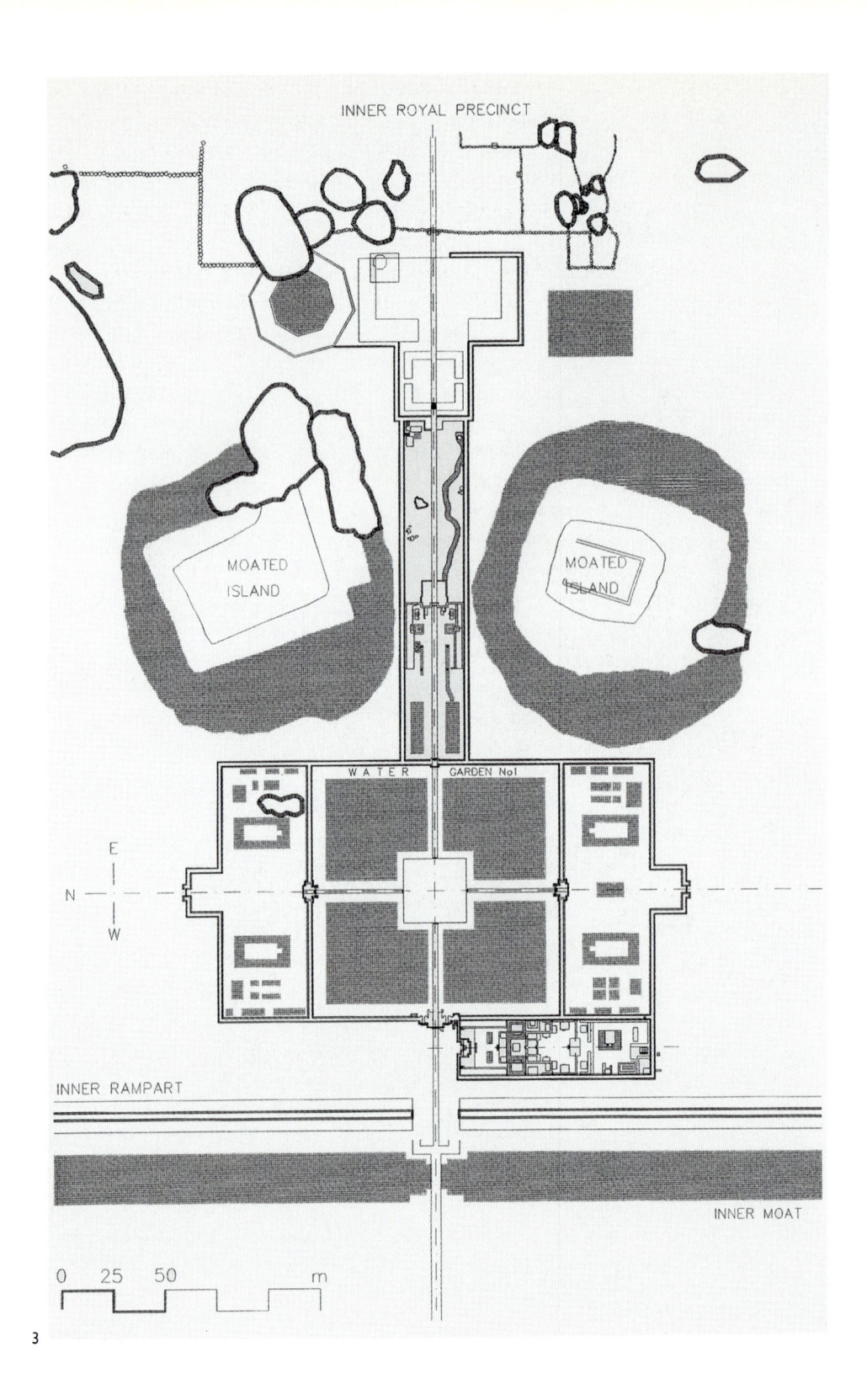

3   N.Cooray *The restoration of the gardens of Sigiriya, Sri Lanka*

pools and ponds, serpentine streams punctuated by fountains, moated islands and numerous other water-retaining structures symmetrically laid out (figs. 3, 5 and 6). All of these waterbodies, including the moats that surround the entire complex, are interconnected by a sophisticated network of underground conduits, aqueducts, canals and so on, fed initially by the great man-made tank to the south of the rock.

The major transverse axis of the complex is formed by a 'char-bagh' feature (water garden no. 1 in figs. 3 and 4) at right angles to the main axis. Here, a large

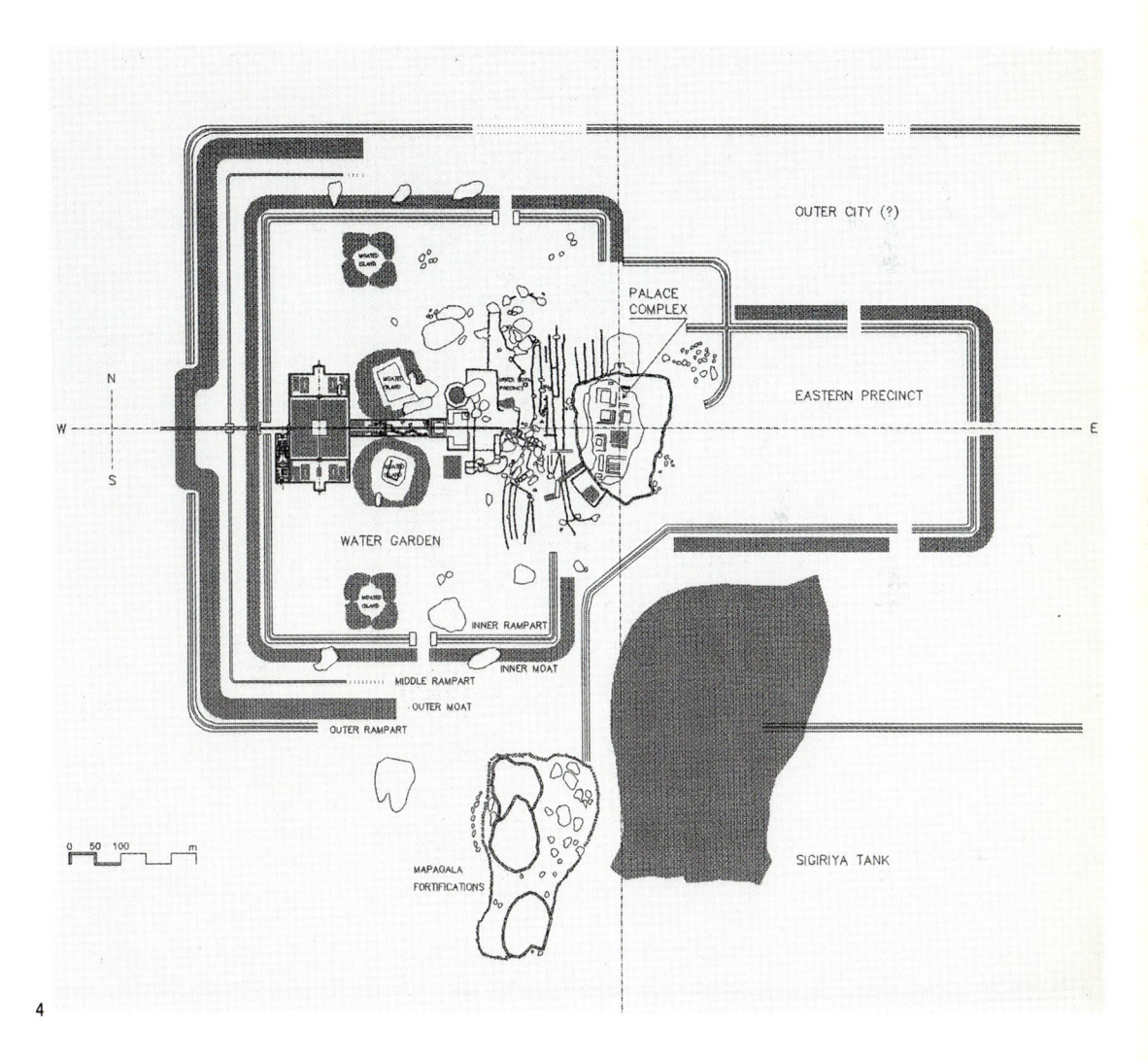

3 Western precinct showing the central axial pathway and the symmetrical layout.
4 The layout of Sigiriya.

moated square island is linked to the main garden by four causeways oriented towards the north, south, east and west respectively. From here, the moat that surrounds the island is separated into four L-shaped ponds. This square island was originally occupied by a large pavilion. There are two more such features located away from the east-west axis, close to the northern and southern ramparts of the western precinct.

This symmetrical and geometrical pleasure garden gradually merges with the organic and asymmetrical garden forms of the hilly terrain associated with the rock (the inner royal precincts). Fashioned into a series of ascending terraces towards the foot of the main rock, this area consists of picturesque natural boulders of various sizes. Nearly all the boulders had a pavilion on top and a plastered and painted cave shelter at the base. Several winding paths and stairways are laid out through the natural arches, alleys, courtyards and so on, formed by clusters of boulders at varying levels, thus presenting a different and exciting spatial experience, towards a landing at the southwestern base of the rock (fig. 7). Compared to the pleasure garden, this garden appears less formal, more intimate and well integrated in the natural landscape.

The access from the landing to the summit of the rock leads at first through a walled serpentine pathway along the western face of the rock, then through a massive brick-built lion-figured staircase and finally through a zigzag stairway constructed along the sheer vertical rock-face of the northern side. Originally, the whole of the western and northern rock-faces above the serpentine pathway was plastered and painted with the famous Sigiriya damsels, only few of which have survived. This painted band, which is nearly 140 metres long and 40 metres wide with damsels carrying flowers, will undoubtedly have provided a dramatic background to the gardens lying below. On the other hand, it must have reduced the boldness of the central rock, and given a soaring and floating effect to the skyward abode of the king. The gardens of Sigiriya were meant to be viewed and experienced not only within the gardens themselves, but also from the palace complex on the summit of the rock. From this vantage point, the thick tropical jungle extending to the horizon provides a matching background to the gardens below.

2 Conservation policy and programme

The conservation work at Sigiriya was begun as far back as 1894, after the establishment of the Department of Archaeology in Sri Lanka. However, this paper will be confined only to the conservation work which is being carried out since 1980, with the commencement of the UNESCO-Sri Lanka project of the Cultural Triangle – the most important systematic garden conservation programme ever undertaken in Sri Lanka.

The essence of the conservation policy and programme adopted and implemented under this project concerns the following.

THE DEGREE OF INTERVENTION   Since any intervention with a monument or site may also lead to its destruction, the policy adopted at the Sigiriya gardens is to leave a considerable part of the gardens untouched for future experts to handle, with the aid of more developed conservation techniques. As the layout of Sigiriya shows a symmetrical pattern on either side of the east-west axis, it was decided to confine the conservation to a single quadrant of the complex. The symmetrical planning will help to visualize the layout of the other side of the axis. Since most of the earlier conservation activities had taken place in the southwest quadrant, that area was selected for the present conservation work. This approach also gives visitors the opportunity to experience the contrast between the untouched areas and monuments north of the east-west axis and the conserved areas and monuments south of it.

5 Aerial view of the western precinct. (Photo: Nilan Cooray)

Since Sigiriya is no longer a living city, the buildings and other structures will not be restored to their original forms. Instead, only the spatial organization of the complex will be conserved by retaining the archaeological or antiquarian character of Sigiriya. However, the necessary pathways, flights of steps and such will be conserved or restored for current use, without destroying the natural setting.

TREATMENT OF THE REMAINS FROM DIFFERENT PERIODS   The site of the Sigiriya gardens had several construction phases from the third century BC onwards. Therefore, in order to avoid possible confusion by conserving the remains from different periods which may be exposed during excavation, only the major construction phase will be conserved and other remains closed after documentation. However, if archaeologically significant earlier and/or later phases are found, segments of such phases will be exposed and conserved to show the vertical history of the site without upsetting its actual layout (fig. 8).

THE FORM OF PLANTING   Unlike the material remains, the planting on historic sites has almost completely disappeared, without leaving any physical trace of its original character. This is a common problem in the conservation of historic gardens, and there is still a lot of debate, research and experimentation going on in this field. The policy adopted at the Sigiriya gardens is not to introduce any form of major planting. However, the existing trees which have grown there through the centuries already give the gardens a certain visual and structural character that should be left untouched. Therefore, every effort is made to retain the existing tree cover at the complex. When trees are found growing within the buildings or on the terraces, they are left alone on an island of earth to protect the roots.[3] Besides, these mounds of earth provide an indication of the layers with which the monuments were buried (fig. 9). The trees that grow on the walls, interrupting the latter's continuity, are also kept and the walls will be connected only when the tree dies.

THE HYDRAULIC SYSTEM   As the western precinct is dominated by such features as ponds, pools, fountains, moats, etc., the ancient hydraulic system will be restored to make them function again. Hence, some of the ancient underground conduits are now restored by de-silting them, which helped to fill some of the conserved water-retaining structures such as the southwest and southeast ponds of water garden no. 1, the pools of water garden no. 2 and the moat around the southern 'summer palace'. Yan-oya, an irrigation canal which

8

6   The main rock from the garden. (Photo: Nilan Cooray)
7   A stairway through a natural arch. (Photo: Nilan Cooray)
8   Treatment of the remains from different periods. Note the flight of steps of an earlier phase to the right of the main flight of steps. (Photo: Nilan Cooray)

flows to the west of the complex, is now tapped to fill the outer moat and at the same time raise the water level within the complex. Moreover, as a first step towards the restoration of the Sigiriya tank – which was the primary source of water to the Sigiriya gardens – a portion of the tank bund extending from the hilly terrain of the Sigiriya complex up to the Mapagala fortifications has now been repaired (fig.10).

DOCUMENTATION   The conservation work of the Sigiriya gardens will be documented at the following stages:
· initial documentation of the situation prior to any intervention
· documentation during and after excavation
· documentation during and after conservation.

Therefore, at the outset the entire Sigiriya complex was surveyed to prepare a contour map at half-metre intervals and to establish a 30-metre grid, planned on north-south and east-west orientations. These grids were marked on the ground by specific bench marks, giving horizontal coordinates and a vertical datum related to the mean sea level. Visible ruins were all plotted. Natural elements such as trees and boulders were marked, indicating their heights. A tree survey was also carried out, giving the variety of each tree, the size of its stem and the canopy. Aerial photographs covering the entire site were taken at the lowest altitude ever flown in Sri Lanka, namely, 1,500 metres.[4]

During and after excavation, documentation is carried out with the aid of photography and photogrammetry, along with normal graphic documentation. A detailed report of the excavations, complete with observations and interpretations, is published every six months. Conservation documentation is done in a similar way, by recording the methods, techniques, materials and treatments used for each individual situation. A detailed report of the conservation work is published every year.

OPERATIONAL STRATEGY AND USE OF MATERIALS AND TECHNIQUES
Due to the possible erosion caused by heavy seasonal rains and the movement of large numbers of visitors around the site, the general strategy adopted in the conservation of the excavated monuments is to commence the conservation work as soon as possible. In the case of ponds, pools, moats and other water-retaining structures, the excavations are planned during the dry season to prevent or minimize the seepage of underground water. To ensure that excavated data are not destroyed by water filling in during the rainy season, every effort is made to conserve them above the highest water level. In the areas through which the pathways for visitors are laid out, the excavations are planned during seasons when visitors to the Sigiriya site are at a minimum. Even then alternative temporary pathways will be provided, avoiding such areas.

Due to the heavy cost of manufacturing ancient-size bricks and other prac-

10

9 A conserved wall with an island of earth to protect the roots of a tree. (Photo: Nilan Cooray)
10 The Sigiriya tank, the primary source of water to the gardens. Note the repaired bund. (Photo: Nilan Cooray)

tical difficulties, engineering bricks were commonly used in the conservation of brickwork prior to the start of the Cultural Triangle Project at Sigiriya. However, modern engineering bricks are much smaller than the ancient bricks found at Sigiriya and do not match with the character of the old brickwork. With the start of this project, it was decided to use purpose-made bricks moulded to the ancient size. These bricks have the Cultural Triangle emblem stamped on them, together with the year of manufacture. Since the ponds, pools, etc. are expected to contain and hold water after conservation, the durability of the submerged conserved brickwork is ensured by increasing the pressure resistance of the purpose-made bricks to 300 p.s.i. and reducing the water absorption rate to 13 per cent.[5]

The conservation of the excavated pathways and flights of steps at Sigiriya is a real challenge. Limestone was commonly used as material for the steps, which are always in a very bad state of preservation when exposed, with some of them missing. Since these steps are intended to be used by the visitors, the missing ones will be reproduced with brick or rubble masonry which is given a limestone effect by using limestone crystals and a mixture of lime and dolomite.

11

12

To make the existing weathered limestone steps durable, they will be treated in the same way and, in addition, sprayed with dolomite-lime water as a protective coating.

MAINTENANCE, PRESENTATION AND VISITOR FACILITIES The maintenance of the whole of the Sigiriya complex at a presentable level is found to be a demanding task, which needs considerable funds as well as strict supervision. The strategy adopted is to divide the Sigiriya gardens into several zones, a high degree of maintenance being required for the eye-catching areas, while maintenance of the less conspicuous zones will be modest.

Owing to the large volume of visitor traffic to the site, there is considerable wear and tear attacking the monuments, especially the pathways and flights of steps. To overcome this problem, experiments are carried out by paving the pathways with rubble, while rendering gravel mixed with lime concrete, in harmony with the antique character of the Sigiriya complex. To make the presentation of Sigiriya more comprehensive, meaningful and attractive, tame animals such as deer and peacocks will be introduced to the park in addition to the natural population of monkeys and birds.[6] Different varieties of fish and crocodiles will be bred in the ponds and moats respectively, the crocodiles once being bred in the moats to prevent the enemy from crossing them.

A suitable floodlight system will also be installed once the conservation and layout programmes are completed.

Since Sigiriya is a famous archaeological site, the large number of visitors dictates the need to improve the existing access facilities, especially to the 'fresco pocket' and the summit of the rock. The present spiral stairway to the 'fresco pocket', erected in 1938, is the only available means to ascend and descend. The one-way traffic flow creates a 'bottleneck' effect, resulting in serious congestion problems during the days of heavy traffic (fig.11). To solve this, an additional spiral staircase will be introduced at the opposite end of the existing one.[7] The steel handrail anchored to the face of the rock was the only safety provision for the visitors who attempted the difficult climb to the top of the rock through the 'lion paws'. In order to have a smooth flow of both upward and downward traffic, two gangways have now been constructed with steel steps resting on the rock (fig.12).

Car parks have been provided close to the western and southern gateways to the complex, with adequate shady parking spaces. Systematically arranged stalls to sell souvenirs and other goods are also erected. A museum to exhibit the special finds unearthed during the excavations will be established, as well as an information centre.

11 The spiral staircase to the 'fresco pocket'. (Photo: Nilan Cooray)

12 The two gangways along the face of the rock. (Photo: Nilan Cooray)

3 Conclusion

As described at the beginning of this paper, the walled-in Sigiriya city is only the nucleus of a greater landscape pattern of the Sigiriya region, with its monastery, its agricultural settlements and their irrigation tanks, the Mapagala fortifications, the great man-made Sigiriya tank, the forest, and so on – all making it a place of very special interest. Therefore, important though it is to conserve the landscape within the moats and ramparts of Sigiriya, the preservation of the landscape beyond it is also a necessity. To this end, the whole of the greater Sigiriya region has now been declared to fall under the country's Urban Development Authority law, which will control the essential features of its landscape and develop the region effectively.[8] Whatever the development plans may be, they should be in harmony with the historical and cultural landscape pattern of the whole region. That is the true spirit of conservation.

---

1 Bandaranayake, 'Sigiriya', p.114.
2 See Bandaranayake, 'Amongst Asia's Earliest Surviving Gardens', pp.3-35; and Ellepola, 'Conjectural Hydraulics of Sigiriya', pp.172-227.
3 Selveratnam and Perera, *Sigiriya Project – 1988*, p.6.
4 Silva, 'The Cultural Triangle', p.191.
5 Selveratnam and Perera, *Sigiriya Project – 1988*, p.4.
6 Silva and Guruge, *The Safeguarding of the Cultural Triangle of Sri Lanka*, p.31.
7 Selveratnam and Perera, *Sigiriya Project – 1988*, p.7.
8 *Development Plan for Sigiriya Heritage City*, vols. I and II.

Bandaranayake, Senake. 'Sigiriya: City, Palace and Royal Gardens'. In *The Cultural Triangle of Sri Lanka*. Paris / Colombo, 1993, pp.112-35.

Bandaranayake, Senake. 'Amongst Asia's Earliest Surviving Gardens: The Royal and Monastic Gardens at Sigiriya and Anuradhapura', in *Historic Gardens and Sites* (Colombo, 1993), pp.3-35.

Development Plan for Sigiriya Heritage City. Vols. I and II. CCF and UDA Publication, 1989.

Ellepola, Chandana. 'Conjectural Hydraulics of Sigiriya'. In *Ancient Ceylon*. Vol. V (Centenary Volume), no.11. Colombo, 1990, pp.172-227.

Selveratnam and Perera. *Sigiriya Project – 1988*. Colombo, 1992.

Silva, Roland. 'The Cultural Triangle: International Safeguarding Campaign'. In *The Cultural Triangle of Sri Lanka*. Paris / Colombo, 1993, pp.176-93.

Silva, Roland, and Ananda W.P. Guruge. *The Safeguarding of the Cultural Triangle of Sri Lanka – Prospects and Progress*. UNESCO and Sri Lanka, n.d.

The seminar: A summary of workshops and discussions
Compiled by Fridy Duterloo, Badeloch Noldus, Sjoerd Schaper, Annegien Schrier and Daphne Thissen

THE FOLLOWING SUMMARY is presented here to preserve some of the content of the discussions during the workshops. For the future historiography of Dutch garden history it seems important to document the different stages and changes in the development of our way of thinking on the restoration and the interpretation of gardens.

1 *Report on the Workshop Cultural Landscape*

CHAIRMEN *Erik de Jong and Kjell Lundquist*
RAPPORTEUR *Annegien Schrier*
PARTICIPANTS *P.A. Bakker, W.C.J. Boer, Ms. L.M.Copijn-Schukking, N.F.C.Hazendonk, E.Kaptein, J.Renes, W.J.A.Snelder, Ms. D.A.Sy-A-Foek, G.Wijesuriya*

The following questions were formulated:
- General: what were the meaning, the position and the image of nature and agriculture in the original context of the garden, and how may the historical combination of nature, agrarian landscape and culture find a meaningful place in the restoration concept?
- What is the potential and what are the shortcomings of the existing landscape if considered in terms of nature, landscape, cultural history and spatial management (inclusive of the quality of the aesthetic image)? To what extent does the restoration plan reinforce or weaken these values?
- What solutions and warnings can be formulated with respect to the restoration/reconstruction?

To break the ice, all participants gave their impression of the garden, after the visit earlier that afternoon. These first impressions turned out to be a good point of reference to establish the essentials of the garden and the surrounding landscape. It was concluded that the differences in height were most characteristic of the location. From the house, the landscape is like a concave space with strong associations of a theatre, while from the surrounding landscape, the house with its terraces looks like the *scena*. The position of the house uses this spatial experience to the full. Set halfway the slope there are at the same time secludedness and protection from the woods behind, as well as openness and freedom of a view that embraces the whole valley. This landscape setting of a country mansion is unique within the territorial borders of the Netherlands. The landscape offers quite a few strong elements: the river Jeker draws the attention by its irregular winding, thus providing a poetic landscape element, the pastures around the garden lend the landscape a distinct agricultural character, while the terraces with fruit-trees point to horticultural activities. It was noted with amazement that the landscape was so unspoilt and breathed such a strong atmosphere.

The discussion of these characteristics soon led to quite a few questions. What, for example, is the historicity of these visual qualities? Which elements have changed in the course of history? How is, and was, the relationship between garden and landscape?

To start with the last question, it proved to be almost impossible to characterize this relationship in terms of the usual contrast between culture (the garden) and nature (the landscape). Attempts to define the different elements in opposite terms of cultural and natural values proved unsuccessful. It became apparent that the whole area is a cultural landscape, with the inclusion of important natural values. In this respect, landscape and garden are a unity, not a contrast. In the course of history, the hand of man has become less explicit and less manifest the more one recedes from the castle as the focus point of culture. Yet, this image may not differ much from the historical situation, when agriculture played an important part in the use of the estate. The detailed geometric garden was an important gradient between the house and the landscape.

It proved to be quite difficult to formulate definite observations. Much information on the situation in the past was lacking, such as data on ownership of the land, use of the soil, the geomorphology. Certain changes in the landscape were obvious. The pastures must have looked differently because of the use of more extensive agricultural methods. There would have been a more varied flora and more trees. The water level must have been much higher than nowadays, which would have had consequences for the diversity of plant species and, possibly, for the course of the Jeker. It is, for example, inconceivable that the access of water to the pond was managed via a dam. Such information could be important for the further restoration plan; it was strongly recommended that further research in these matters is to be undertaken.

The second meeting tried to evaluate what could be done by way of an actual restoration. This discussion centred on the degree of possible and desired intervention. Different gradations were seen to be possible, varying from minimal (doing nothing) to maximum (a full reconstruction) intervention. The aim would be to find an optimal solution, which would cause as little destruction of historic material as possible and, at the same time, a maximum reinforcement of existing qualities: a so-called win-win situation. A complete reconstruction was seen as undesirable due to the lack of historical data. What, indeed, is there to restore or to reconstruct? Drastic changes would create an abrupt break in historical continuity. During the excursion to Hex, everybody noticed the value of a continuous development. The many historical layers all represent their own values.

As a result of these observations, the area of the Jeker valley was divided into different zones: a first and outer zone, defined as the landscape of the valley proper; a second in-between zone, the cultural landscape, comprising elements of landscape and culture; and a third, central zone, the detailed landscape of the garden. It was noted that, since the borders between these zones are not absolute, the integrity and unity of landscape and garden would be guaranteed, while at the same time each of these zones might be approached differently. Thus, the degree of intervention might differ per zone.

The differences between the zones are determined by the cultural component showing more or less of its effects in the landscape. Now the whole landscape is to be regarded as a cultural landscape, and as such it shows man's hand everywhere. There are, however, still some subtle gradations to be observed. The castle with its terraces is the most 'cultural', even if for its garden 'natural' elements have been used. In this central zone, the gradations could be made visible by bringing the first terrace more in relation with the castle. Changes in layout and choice of materials could shape it more into an outdoor room. On the second and third terraces, the old structural elements of paths, parterres and fountain could be revealed while at the same time striving for an effective simplicity, which in the choice of plants and architecture would still do justice to the artful and ornamental character of this part of the garden. So a harmonious transition would develop towards the second zone, which is characterized by a combination of horticulture and agriculture. The vineyard, the existing fruit-trees (to be enhanced and replanted in a future maintenance scheme), the pastures and the pond on the fourth terrace (restored without the trees) are representative elements in this zone. The Cannerweg could be lowered by about thirty centimetres to its original level. The third, outer zone, the landscape proper, was used for extensive agriculture, contrary to its present use. Yet, less cattle in the valley and more flora and fauna, as part of an ecological programme, will enrich the natural values in the Jeker valley. To what extent new avenues will have to be planted remains therefore to be seen: when the Jeker valley is to be developed as a wet, ecological, landscape, with its own beauty, one should opt for combining this natural development with a simple consolidation of the pond, in order to show it as a remnant of the former terrace. Seen from the castle, it could play its role as part of a view that enables us to discover the transition from formal to less formal. Thus, an old theme is being renewed, doing justice to new insights, tastes and desires.

More research is still needed to add to our knowledge of the course of the Jeker, the avenues of trees along the pond (were there any?), the location of the Sterrebos and the dating of the farmhouse on the main axis: they all represent important elements for future decision making.

2 Report on the Workshop Archaeology and Infrastructure

CHAIRMEN *W. Dijkman and P.-A. Lablaude*
RAPPORTEUR *Ms. F. Duterloo*
PARTICIPANTS *Ms. E. Cattarini Leger, N. Cooray, Ms. B. van Hellenberg Hubar, H.C.H. Knook, S.E. Minis, F.J.D. Mulder, B. Olde Meierink, C. Oostwegel*

Three questions were formulated to provide a frame of reference and to determine the content of the workshop:
- What physical elements and structures of the eighteenth-century gardens and terraces can be defined above the ground, below the ground and at ground level, by means of archaeological and architectural research?
- To what extent can or must these be restored or presented as part of the reconstruction of the gardens, and how does this relate to the dilemma of preserving the archaeological artefacts and the authenticity of the restoration of the gardens?
- What solutions and warnings can be formulated with respect to the restoration/reconstruction assignment?

The workshop had two meetings during which, by provoking a discussion, the answers to the above questions were to be formulated. The conclusions drawn in the workshop could then be shared with the other workshops in the final session.

At the opening of the first meeting, it was not entirely clear to the members of the workshop what was actually to be achieved. Although the above questions were to be answered, everybody agreed that it was difficult to discuss the actual future of the Neercanne garden, since there is the problem of the divided ownership.

Mr. Oostwegel, who owns the land around the castle north of the road, wants to restore the baroque garden to its former glory, but he does not intend to make it into a commercial funfair. It will be open to the public and the plan is based on an average of 30,000 visitors a year, for whom there is enough parking space in the existing car park.

The foundation Het Limburgs Landschap owns the land at the other side of the road, where the large pond is. Though invited, they did not send a representative to explain their views and ideas on the future of this historic landscape. Nevertheless, the workshop decided to try to include the ideas expressed earlier by Het Limburgs Landschap – namely, to create an ecologically balanced landscape – into the final advice.

The archaeological excavations at Neercanne garden, so Ir. Knook concluded, showed one historical layer, dating from the eighteenth century. On the strength of the findings of the excavation, it is possible, according to Knook, to restore the baroque garden.

In trying to define what (garden) archaeology is and what kind of methods – such as the actual excavation, stratigraphy, botanical analysis, dendrochronology, etc. – are used, members strongly disagreed among themselves as to the definition of archaeology and what its aims are.

In general, most members had not been informed well enough on the actual archaeological research done at Neercanne and, besides, they were not aware of the latest, highly advanced (non-destructive) methods used in garden archaeology today. This made the discussion even more difficult. We all agreed, though, that if we want to reconstruct the past, we should include all the historical layers and decide why certain structures were built. The main problem with practical archaeology is that it, more often than not, destroys the evidence; documentation made during excavation is all that is left. Most of the time, archaeology asks more questions than it can answer. But it can still give information – as, for example, on the designed patterns of a formal parterre.

The next point made was that if one wants to outline a good conservation strategy (including further archaeological research) for the Neercanne Castle garden and its surrounding historic and natural landscape, it can be very helpful to consult the internationally accepted guidelines for the conservation of historic gardens as expressed by the International Council on Monuments and Sites (ICOMOS) in the Florence Charter of 1981, in the revised Burra Charter of 1988 and in the Venice Charter of 1966.

It was also put forward that, when restoring a garden, one should make a clear scenario rather than a scenario full of compromises, as was the case with the famous and infamous restoration of the St. Servaas Church in Maastricht.

A substantial contribution to the workshop was made by Mr. Pierre Lablaude, Chef des Monuments Historiques at Versailles. By showing and explaining the strategy of one of his earlier restoration projects of a garden in a village near Paris, he pointed out the dangers of a total reconstruction. Part of the restoration was the actual rebuilding (reconstruction) of follies and other structures. For the broderie parterres, where no traces were found of the actual design, a pattern was chosen which was fashionable at the time the château was built. Lablaude, now unhappy about this restoration, suggested that it is sometimes better not to rebuild certain structures, even though you know they are there (for example, because of evidence below the ground). A total reconstruction or 'restoration in spirit' does not have to be 'wrong', said Lablaude, but it can cause a pastiche effect and consequently the garden looses its authenticity. However, he concluded, one must never forget that restoring a garden is like performing a piece of music; it will always be a personal interpretation.

Lablaude also explained that existing 'hardware' in a garden – built structures such as follies, garden walls, fountains, etc. – does not change or disappear as fast as the 'software' – the vegetation. Trees and other plants change because they grow and will of course eventually die. Lablaude advised that it is highly necessary to make a management plan for the conservation of Neercanne garden, with an extensive planting scheme that 'thinks ahead', covering at least the next five years or more.

The final conclusion of the meeting was that there are three different conservation strategies possible as far as the archaeological remains at Neercanne are concerned: *1* total reconstruction; *2* consolidation of the remains (minimal intervention); *3* no intervention at all (not recommended by the workshop).

Most members agreed that the garden and its surrounding landscape have to be treated as one concept. If one does not restore it, one will miss a fine opportunity to preserve this concept for future generations. All the members of the workshop agreed that immediate action has to be taken at Neercanne garden, before the structural evidence above and under the ground, such as the large pond, will disappear or be completely destroyed. The option of 'leaving the site as it is' was not favoured by any of the members.

The second meeting of the workshop can be characterized as much more efficient. The members were better informed about the archaeological excavations taking place at Neercanne and they were familiar with the new methods used in garden archaeology, such as shown at Hampton Court.

Furthermore, the workshop was informed by Mr. Minis, of the Municipality of Maastricht, about the woods (Cannerberg) behind Neercanne Castle. There the remains (above ground) are found of the obelisk, the theatre and other buildings. There are also traces of the original layout of the paths and several old trees. It was concluded that the historical research, especially as regards this part of the garden, has been completely neglected up to now. The workshop agreed that a total survey of the area is necessary, including both the garden and its wider landscape. This survey should be made by a small group of people from different disciplines. As to the methodology and the focal point of the survey, other surveys made of historic gardens and landscapes could be used as examples.

Part of the survey should deal with the different historical layers of Neercanne Castle itself. This should be led by a prominent monuments archaeologist.

It was made clear that, due to limited financial means and lack of time, the archaeological research of the Neercanne garden concentrated on the structural elements as seen in the historic engravings of the garden. All agreed that if there is going to be a second archaeological research at Neercanne, it should extend to the whole area, including the woods behind the castle. A profound geomorphological and stratigraphic research is necessary, as well as an extensive pollen analysis. Trees should be identified, dated and 'mapped'.

The first terrace, where no archaeological excavations have taken place, should be considered when there is going to be a restoration of the garden. This can cause a problem because today the terrace functions as part of the restaurant, and Mr. Oostwegel would like to keep it that way in the plans for the future.

The fourth terrace requires specific and precise archaeological research. Decisive factors regarding the design of the garden and the creation of the landscape are the history of the course of the river and the actual layout of the roads. First of all, the pond and other already uncovered structures should be consolidated. Next comes a non-destructive geodesic measurement of the whole area, which could be done by a student. The excavation itself should be 'teaspoon archaeology'. It might also be worthwhile to check old aerial photographs (maybe from the Second World War collection in Wageningen). The area, including historic houses in Kanne, should also be checked for *spolia*, reused stone material, from the garden. And it was found important, when possible, to restore certain viewpoints, such as from the woods, the Cannerberg and from the castle, towards the Maas valley.

3 *Report on the Workshop Planting Schemes and Maintenance*

CHAIRMAN *J. Woudstra*
RAPPORTEURS *Ms. B. Noldus and Ms. D. M. I. Thissen*
PARTICIPANTS *Ms. L. H. Albers, H. Boers, Th. A. P. van den Bosch, M. Laird, Duchess N. Michel d'Ursel, I. Jansen, Ms. C. Oldenburger-Ebbers, Ms. J. van Schaik, H. M. J. Tromp, Ms. S. E. van Weede-van Nievelt, W. Zieleman*

The questions raised by the organization for this group to work on were:
- Which natural and artificial elements form the basis of the original concept, and to what extent are they based on local, regional or foreign factors and influences?
- Is it possible and preferable to reconstruct the historic views and planting schemes or would a more modern design with present-day colours, forms and plants be more appropriate?
- What recommendations and warnings can be formulated with regard to the possible restoration/reconstruction of the garden?

The discussion started by dealing with the questions raised after the introductory talks and walk round the garden. All the members of the group, on that first night, felt that there was insufficient information available, certainly not enough to start a possible restoration/reconstruction programme. The consensus of opinion in the group was that more research (of all aspects of the garden) was required. The article by K. Brummel[1] shows that the reconstruction plans are mainly based on an eighteenth-century poem written by F. Halma and commissioned by the then owner D.W. van Dopff, and on the archaeological research which was carried out by people of the Technical University Delft in 1989. The print which illustrates the poem is the only pictorial historical source, yet such prints are known for their idealizing of the actual site. This makes the print a dubious source which could lead to several possible, and conflicting, suggestions and/or interpretations. The second and third days of the conference (the seminar and the excursion) were regarded as highly successful and important, although the overall view on how to approach the gardens of Neercanne Castle had not changed. The first night, the group had requested more detailed information from the archaeologist (Mr. Knook, TU Delft) who gave a talk on his research of the garden that Friday afternoon. Again this had little effect on the general opinion in the group. The members felt that further preparatory research would be necessary before future restoration work could be considered. Following on Mr. Knook's talk, the group discussed the available information on the main issues and prepared their recommendations and warnings.

The recommendations were the following. The group suggested the formation of a research team consisting of, among others, an archaeologist, an architect and a botanical historian, who should concentrate on their particular disciplines in the restoration. This team should remain actively involved throughout the project and, at a later stage, supervise the maintenance work.

For future research and planting/maintenance schemes, it was recommended that non-destructive methods should be implemented at the appropriate time of year.

For the different terraces the group recommended the following:
- the fourth terrace: removal of all trees around the pond (these are destructive to the pond) and restoration of the pond
- the third terrace: no more sheep-grazing; restoration of the fountain; replacement of sculpture only if enough evidence on position, character, iconography, height, etc. is available; raising the level of soil in order to protect the historical layer(s) and to prepare the ground for flower-beds; possible planting scheme for the garden wall: hop plants
- the second terrace: restoration as a walking area; there is ample opportunity to add wall-plants
- the first terrace: leave as found, possibility to use plants in pots
- the Sterrebos: there is not much known about this wood, but without doubt it was an important part of the estate and is therefore unsuitable for use as a car park, etc.

If further research would only yield scanty extra data and insufficient information on the eighteenth-century garden for a proper restoration plan, the group suggested reconstruction on a modest scale. Some significant surviving elements of the baroque garden, such as the fountain and the pond, could be restored and incorporated in a new, modern garden scheme. This type of reconstruction would have to be carried out in accordance with the scale and proportions of the existing garden, while recognizing the function of the house and the importance of the archaeology with respect to the wider landscape. It was further suggested that an ornamental kitchen-garden scheme should complement the important agricultural aspect of the estate.

The working group listed the following warnings:
- simulation should be avoided in a possible future reconstruction
- if reconstruction is prolonged, the grounds should be covered by soil for protection
- a list should be prepared of destructive plants which must not be used in the garden (destructive to the wall, the historical layers, etc.).

The working group drew up the following summary in conclusion. Due to the lack of information, recommendations cannot be given concerning factors which might have influenced the original concept. Within a delicate reconstruction scheme, the essence of the original design layout can be rejuvenated. Careful selection of new species for planting should further complement the reconstruction.

4 Report on the Workshop Geometrical Design and Architecture

CHAIRMEN G. Hajós and B. Kwast
RAPPORTEUR J. Schaper
PARTICIPANTS J.C. Bierens de Haan, W.A. Diedenhofen, M. van Gessel, Ms. F. Hopper Boom, U.M. Mehrtens, C.J. van der Peet, F.W. van Voorden

The questions pertinent to this workshop were put as follows:
- Which principles of design can be formulated in the construction of the terraces and garden, both for the component parts and for the design as a whole? To what extent is the interaction between the (historical) geomorphological arrangement and the (original) design of the garden to be perceived in the existing landscape? Which structures and elements are sufficiently authentic to warrant restoration and which could be used for a contemporary landscape design?
- What solutions and warnings can be formulated with respect to the restoration/reconstruction?

At the start of the first session, chairman Mr. Hajós requested the participants to reflect upon the existing ensemble and single out some of its individual characteristics.

The sensitive relation between the house and the first three terraces was stressed; the presence of two bastions, instead of a direct connection, between the first and second terraces, as well as the strong transverse axis of the third, were marked out as distinguishing features. The majority of the participants appreciated the present, romantic beauty of the fourth terrace, enhanced by its separate position opposite the Cannerweg.

While some structural elements of the original gardens remain, all ornamental elements are lost. Any attempt to reconstruct the ensemble as shown in Le Bruyn's engraving will therefore provide us with a kind of 'Disneyland baroque' – history manipulated to supply a cheap kind of attractiveness for the sake of money.

Instead of striving towards a unified garden preservation scheme, i.e., the reconstruction of only one historic phase, the participants agreed that contradictions in the gardens (various historic traces) should be accepted – as if dealing with stone-built heritage. Thus, the age of the gardens and their accumulated history were considered as major values. The insertion of a small museological part, in which excavations are shown and where a part of the parterre is reconstructed, might supplement the didactic value of the gardens.

The second session took place after a visit to the exemplarily maintained eighteenth-century private terraced gardens at Hex (Belgium), whose impressive pureness might be held up as an example. During this session, each of the participants reflected upon the main values of the Neercanne gardens. These were filed under the headings 'Site' and 'View'. Elements of the former category are the memory of the consecutive proprietors, the interplay of artificial (geometrical/architectural) and natural (terraced morphology) elements, the presence of running water, viz. the river Jeker, and the survival of the original baroque gardens under a layer of soil. Examples of the latter category are the unspoiled beauty of the surrounding valley, the aged and timeless aspect of the house and the impressive garden walls – by their height unique in the Netherlands – and the influence of the ensemble upon the landscape.

Taking these values into account, the participants formulated their recommendations, trying to find the best way to preserve the remaining structural elements of the gardens (the borderlines, the two ponds and the hidden dykes at the fourth terrace).

The first terrace is a restaurant terrace, it can't therefore be made gardenesque but might be redesigned as a continuous platform. The second terrace forms an ecological territory in unity with the walls, only espaliers (e.g. grapes or fruit-trees) over a grass floor might be reinserted there.

Provided that the pond will be restored and the soil left untouched, the third terrace might be redesigned either as an ornamental vegetable garden or as a 'garden theatre' where excavations are shown and unobtrusive topiary or modest reconstruction of a part of the parterre might be carried out; it is also a fit place for garden exhibitionss. The terrace's transverse axis might be enhanced.

At the fourth terrace, natural and historical values must be kept in equilibrium; a full reconstruction is ruled out in advance. The pond ought to be protected from further decay, but the outlines of the terrace may be enhanced by restrained redressing only after careful ecologic and archaeologic examination.

The northern terraces, to the right of the house, should preferably be redesigned as vegetable gardens, vineyards or orchards. Finally, further research is necessary to trace the former paths of the slope with the Sterrebos and its belvedere. Considering the wood's ecological value, great care must be used here.

Authenticity and prudence appeared to be this workshop's keywords.

5 Conclusions

Friday evening these results were presented to a Forum, including W. Denslagen (restoration criticism and ethics), J. Houwen (regional planning), T. J. D. Mulder (nature and landscape conservation), W. J. Snelder and E. Kaptein (landscape architecture) and J. Oostwegel (owner of Neercanne). It was a most exhilarating experience to see that all workshop members, who were very much searching for answers in the most diverse ways as possible during the workshops on Wednesday, attained conclusions on more or less the same lines after having heard the lectures on Thursday, and having visited the gardens of Hex, both occasions giving ample opportunity for discussion and further thought. All four workshops found common ground in the need for more research, the reservation towards a total and precise reconstruction and the emphasis on the need to see garden and landscape as a whole, based on the experience and value of the present beauty of the situation. During the informal discussion afterwards, a profound discussion on the ecological nature values of the Jeker valley as relating to the presence of the pond as part of the former garden as a distinct cultural element, even led to the conclusion that both could be seen as inclusive of a future development of the fourth terrace. That is, on the condition that only the pond is to be restored, functioning as a contrasting and historic element within the pastures and the nature area along the river Jeker, yet at the same time playing its part in the view from the terraces. Not only as an exercise, but also in its results, the workshop therefore ended on the hopeful note that it is indeed possible to find agreement among the most different disciplines. The session ended with the expectation that the owner and the Neercanne Castle Gardens Foundation would follow up on the thoughts, ideas and insights proposed by all participants during these three inspiring days.

Let us conclude these summaries of the discussions with the following note by Wil J. A. Snelder, project architect at Blaauboer Kragten Snelder, Garden and

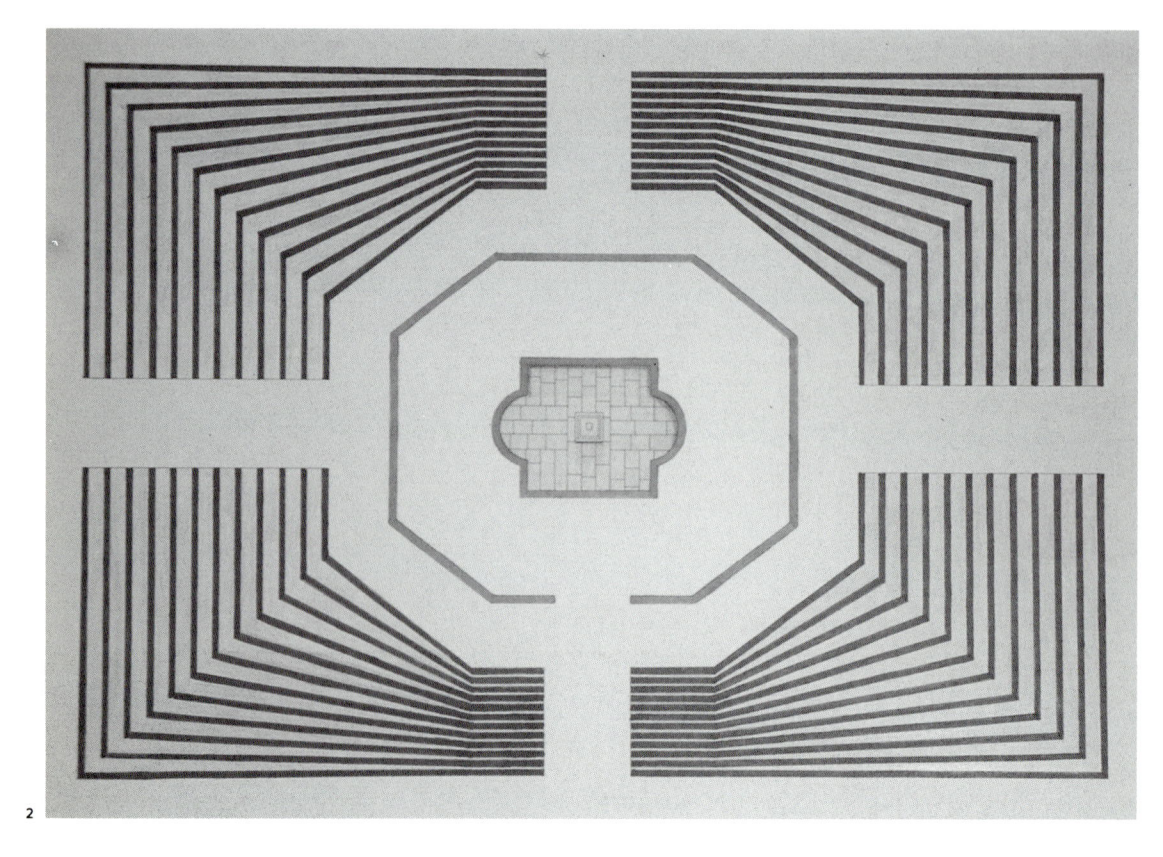

F. Duterloo et al. *The seminar: A summary of workshops and discussions*

Landscape Architects in Roermond and responsible for the final plans of the restoration, on the first phase of the work on the second and third terraces which will be completed in the spring of 1997.

6 WIL J.A.SNELDER *Note on the plans for the second and third terraces*

In accordance with the nearly unanimous conclusion reached at the International Conference on Neercanne in September 1995, a restoration plan has been drawn up which will respect the archaeological data of the earlier garden. The layer of soil containing these data will be left undisturbed.

The renewal of the garden will be restricted to not much more than a restoration of the main structure. This is the only aspect of the garden for which archaeological and historical research produced enough concrete evidence to make a faithful reconstruction possible. To consolidate the existing layers of soil on the two terraces without affecting their current composition, earth will be neither added to the site as a whole nor removed from it. The balance should be zero. Any earth dug out as the paths are reinforced will be spread out over the terrain or incorporated into the parterres.

Thus making use of the removed earth means that the level of the renewed garden will be such that the archaeological evidence can remain intact in its layer of soil beneath the surface. In fact, the new garden will be built on top of the old one. Only in the central section will the original level be maintained, since here the excavated stone-rimmed fountain forms the focal point of the garden. After its repair it will be incorporated into the reconstructed main structure.

With the help of the data obtained through the archaeological investigation, which was conducted on approximately one quarter of the third terrace, a scale drawing was made of this part. Then, on the basis of extrapolation from the location of the north-south and east-west axes and the engraving by Le Bruyn, another scale drawing was made of the entire third terrace (fig. 1). The archaeological research had revealed that the top layer of the paths consisted at the time of a fine-grained, yellow material – probably marl that had been ground or broken up into small pieces.

The colour of the material is very important for the total aspect of the garden's layout. Yellow goes well with the colour of the terrace walls and it accentuates the geometric pattern of the main structure. For this reason, the reconstructed paths will be finished off with *gravier d'or*. The parterres of

1 Wil J.A. Snelder, project architect at Blaauboer Kragten Snelder, Garden and Landscape Architects in Roermond. Scale drawing of the third terrace, on the basis of extrapolation from the location of the north-south and east-west axes and the engraving by Le Bruyn, 1996.

2 Wil J.A. Snelder, project architect at Blaauboer Kragten Snelder, Garden and Landscape Architects in Roermond. Design for the parterres surrounding the central fountain, 1996.

the restored main structure will be bordered by a box hedge with layered box pyramids or cones at the corners. This is in keeping with the information contained in the Le Bruyn engraving and with late-seventeenth-century practice.

The parterres will be filled in with lawn. Too little evidence is available to suggest doing anything else. Moreover, grass will not draw attention away from the main structure, which is the essence of the third terrace.

Le Bruyn's engraving suggests that the parterres surrounding the central fountain were filled in with box cut in the form of a fleur-de-lis. The information provided by the engraving is too unclear, however, to warrant duplication in a specific configuration in the renewed garden. For the total look of the third terrace, however, it is essential that these areas be filled in. It was decided that this should be done in an obviously modern way so as to avoid any falsification of history (fig. 2).

1 Klazien Brummel, '«Natuur met kunst vereent»; historisch onderzoek naar de vroeg 18e-eeuwse situatie van de terrastuin van Kasteel Neercanne', in *Bulletin KNOB*, 92 (1993), 4, pp. 89-114.

Programme of the international conference and lists of specialists attending the conference

WEDNESDAY 27 SEPTEMBER 1995 *The restoration of the baroque gardens of Neercanne Castle, organized by the Netherlands Committee for UNESCO and the Foundation Neercanne Castle Gardens*

13.00–14.00 Arrival at Neercanne Castle of the participants; visit to the gardens guided by H. Knook
14.00–16.00 Plenary session: Welcome by C. Oostwegel / Introduction by F.W. van Voorden / Introduction to the themes of the workshops: cultural landscape (E. de Jong), archaeology and infrastructure (W. Dijkman), planting schemes and maintenance (C. Oldenburger-Ebbers), geometrical designs and architecture (B. Kwast)
16.00–17.00 Visit to the gardens guided by H. Knook
17.00–20.00 Workshops: Cultural Landscape (E. de Jong and K. Lundquist), Archaeology and Infrastructure (W. Dijkman and P.-A. Lablaude), Planting Schemes and Maintenance (C.S. Oldenburger-Ebbers and M. Laird / H.M.J. Tromp and J. Woudstra), Geometrical Design and Architecture (B. Kwast and G. Hajós)
20.00 Dinner at Neercanne Castle

THURSDAY 28 SEPTEMBER 1995 *Public Seminar on the restoration of gardens in Europe and Sri Lanka, held in the Treaty Room of the Provincial Government of Limburg at Maastricht*

10.30 Welcome and opening: D.A. Sy-A-Foek (UNESCO Commission), B.J.M. Baron van Voorst tot Voorst (Governor of the Province of Limburg), E. Cattarini Leger (UNESCO), G. Leibbrandt (UNESCO Commission), F.W. van Voorden (Chair of the Day)
10.45–12.45 E. de Jong: The restoration of Neercanne and the Dutch tradition of gardens; P.-A. Lablaude: The restoration of the Versailles gardens; J. Woudstra: The design of the parterre at Hampton Court; M. Laird: Restoration projects of 17th- and 18th-century gardens in Western Europe
14.00–15.15 C. Oostwegel: Neercanne; G. Hajós: Restoration projects of 17th- and 18th-century gardens in Central Europe; K. Lundquist: Restoration of 17th- and 18th-century gardens and cultural landscapes in Sweden

15.45–16.30 G.Wijesuriya: Introduction on the UNESCO programme in Sri Lanka; N.Cooray: Restoration of the gardens of Sigiriya, Sri Lanka
17.00–18.00 Reception
20.30–22.00 Workshops

FRIDAY 29 SEPTEMBER 1995 *The restoration of the baroque gardens of Neercanne Castle / Workshops at Vaeshartelt Castle*

08.00–13.00 Excursion to Hex gardens in Belgium; reception and guided tour by Countess Michel d'Ursel and her family
13.00–14.00 Lunch at Hex Castle
14.00–20.00 Continuation of the workshops at Vaeshartelt Castle, including a special lecture by H.Knook on the archaeological evidence
20.00–21.30 Presentation of the results of the workshops; Forum discussion, with, on the forum: W.Denslagen (restoration criticism and ethics), J.Houwen (regional planning), T.J.D.Mulder (nature and landscape conservation), C.Oostwegel (owner), W.J.A.Snelder (landscape architecture), E.Kaptein (landscape architecture)
21.30 Closure of the conference

Lists of specialists attending the conference

WORKSHOP CULTURAL LANDSCAPE

P.A.Bakker *Society for the Preservation of Nature in the Netherlands (Natuurmonumenten)*
W.C.J.Boer *Garden and landscape architect*
Ms. L.M.Copijn-Schukking *Copijn Utrecht, groenadviseurs BV, landscape architect*
N.F.C.Hazendonk *Ministry of Agriculture, landscape architect*
E. de Jong *Department for Architectural and Landscape History, Free University, Amsterdam*
E.Kaptein *Office of Blaauboer, Kragten and Snelder, landscape architect*
K.Lundquist *Swedish University of Agricultural Sciences, Department of Landscape Planning*
J.Renes *DLO Winand Staring Centre, Wageningen, social geographer*
Ms. A.Schrier *Rapporteur, student in architectural and landscape history, Free University, Amsterdam*

W.J.A.Snelder *Office of Blaauboer, Kragten and Snelder, restoration architect*
Ms. D.A.Sy-A-Foek *National Commission for UNESCO*
G.Wijesuriya *Director of Conservation, Department of Archaeology, Sri Lanka*

WORKSHOP ARCHAEOLOGY AND INFRASTRUCTURE

N.Cooray *Department of Archeology, Sri Lanka*
W.Dijkman *Municipality of Maastricht, archaeologist*
Ms. F.Duterloo *Rapporteur, garden historian, MA in conservation studies, York*
Ms. B.Hellenberg Hubar *Limburg Monuments Commission*
H.C.H.Knook *Technical University Delft, Faculty of Architecture*

P.-A. Lablaude *Architect and Chef des Monuments Historiques, Château de Versailles*
Ms. E. Cattarini Leger *UNESCO, Section of Cultural Identities*
B. Olde Meierink *SB4, Landscape architects, art historian*
S. E. Minis *Municipality of Maastricht, Monuments Commission*
F. J. D. Mulder
C. Oostwegel *Neercanne Castle, owner*

WORKSHOP PLANTING SCHEMES AND MAINTENANCE

Ms. L. H. Albers *Albers Adviezen*
H. Boers *State Museum Muiderslot*
Th. A. P. van den Bosch *Tree nursery 'De Gaardenhof'*
I. Janssen *Atelier Wilg, landscape architect*
M. Laird *Garden historian, Toronto, Canada*
Ms. B. Noldus *Rapporteur, student in architectural and landscape history, Free University, Amsterdam*
Ms. C. S. Oldenburger-Ebbers *Curator Special Collections Library Agricultural University*
Ms. J. M. van Schaik *Unie van Bosgroepen*
Ms. D. Thissen *Rapporteur, student in architectural and landscape history, State University, Groningen*

H. M. J. Tromp *Stichting Particuliere Historische Buitenplaatsen, historian*
Countess Michel d'Ursel *Hex Castle, Belgium*
Ms. S. E. van Weede-van Nievelt *Bingerden Castle*
J. Woudstra *University of Sheffield, garden historian and landscape restoration architect*
W. Zieleman *State Museum 'Paleis Het Loo'*

WORKSHOP GEOMETRICAL DESIGN AND ARCHITECTURE

J. C. Bierens de Haan *Curator Gelderland Trust for Historic Houses, art historian*
W. A. Diedenhofen *Garden historian, Cleves*
M. van Gessel *Bureau B & B, Amsterdam, landscape architect*
G. Hajós *Hofburg-Schweizerhof Bundesdenkmalamt, Referat für historische Gartenanlagen*
Ms. F. Hopper Boom *Garden historian, Hengelo*
B. Kwast *Technical University Delft, Faculty of Architecture*
U. M. Mehrtens *State Department for Conservation, Zeist*
C. J. van der Peet *State Building Office, The Hague*
S. Schaper *Rapporteur, student in architectural and landscape history, Free University, Amsterdam*
F. W. van Voorden *Technical University Delft, Faculty of Architecture, professor of conservation studies*